Strands

An Apprenticeship with Grief and Loss

Patricia Wild

BARCLAY PRESS
Newberg, OR 97132

Strands
An Apprenticeship with Grief and Loss
©2025 by Patricia Wild

All rights reserved. No part may be reproduced
for any commercial purpose by any method without
permission in writing from the copyright holder.

Barclay Press, Inc.
Newberg, Oregon
www.barclaypress.com

Interior design by Mareesa Fawver Moss
Cover image and design by Eric Muhr

ISBN 978-1-59498-167-8

For my mother

Contents

Preface 7
The Materials of Grief 13
Car Talk 21
Forgotten Ancestors 31
Grief Work Is Soul Work 39
Like Something out of Dickens 51
Deepening 65
With Hope Yet with Tears 95
Just like Your Mother 115
In a Minor Key 129
The next Buddha will be a Sangha. 149
Baked Right In 179
Deepening, Attending, Listening 185
Swirl 205
Appendix A 209
Appendix B 215
Appendix C 221
Acknowledgments 223
Notes from Text 229
Notes from Illustrations 237

Naveo Credit Union windows,
Somerville, Massachusetts, June 2021

Preface

[Labor Day/Rosh Hashanah 2021:] On the twenty-first day of the twenty-first week of the twenty-first year of the twenty-first century, I received news worthy of such auspicious timing. Eric Muhr, publisher of Barclay Press, called to tell me the press would publish *Strands*. To contextualize that momentous call, four days earlier, for the first time in fifteen months, I left my mask on my bureau and my hand sanitizer in my shoulder bag and, fully-vaccinated, stepped outside into a glorious May morning in Somerville, Massachusetts. My neighborhood's lilac bushes still in bloom and scenting the warm air, a mockingbird offered a virtuoso performance atop the triple-decker building across the street. (Was it my imagination, or had that clever bird returned to its pre-lockdown riffs on car alarms and grating metal?)

Gritty bird-sound, abundant spring, naked face—it was all too much. An inner voice shrieked, "Go home; you forgot something. Wrong, wrong, wrong!" as I trudged a block up the street to mail some letters. Touching the mailbox's metal handle with my bare hand, I froze. I *had* forgotten something! (Would vigorous handwashing later be enough?)

Still unsettled, I stopped to smell a neighbor's lilacs. In that direct, maskless, nose-to-blossom moment, I heard another inner voice; this time it was my efficient mother. "I do stop to smell the roses, Patricia," she reminded me. "I just smell them faster than most people!" My friend Minga's commentary on last year's grim spring came to mind: "Death is all around us, and spring has never been so amazing!"

Since that scented day, I've hugged all six grandchildren, traveling by plane to Duluth, Minnesota, in order to hug the youngest, Amy, age four, whom I hadn't hugged in two years. I've again worshipped at Friends Meeting at Cambridge and, masked, experienced Spirit moving through that spacious meetinghouse, through me.

But as I gradually resumed my blessed and easeful life, I started to worry: post-pandemic, would my friends and I, who'd taken turns declaring, "When this is over, we can't go back to normal," do just that? Ensconced in cushy normal again, would we forget our earnest declaration? Would I someday spot a dusty picture of George Floyd still displayed in someone's front window and think, "Oh, right. We'd meant to do something about that!" Would we never "get to the doing part," as my friend and civil rights pioneer, Dr. Lynda Woodruff, had urged?

But my fears were misplaced—no, not about racial justice; they're real, justified, ongoing, and, yes, shared by many other white people. Like the young man on Facebook recently, who, after hearing the pandemic platitude, "We're all in the same boat," for the umpteenth time, vehemently disagreed: "No! We're all in the same *storm*. But we're in different boats. And some of those boats are crappy!"

No, I was wrong about normal. About returning to normal. For *this* isn't over, is it? This ever-morphing, global pandemic continues. Delta rages. Mu lurks. And after this past summer's brutal droughts, floods, heat waves, violent storms, and wildfires, to me it's pretty clear: normal is no more.

I had been in Duluth when this painful realization hit me. Pristine, far-north, located at the edge of the world's largest freshwater lake, Duluth has always seemed to me, well, protected from climate disruption. But in July, while my husband and I visited, wildfire smoke from Canada blanketed that part of the world, already experiencing a serious drought, for two poor-air-quality days. Looking down from our rental's living room window at a thick, gray, ominous, voluminous cloud where the compact city and Lake Superior used to be, I sadly quoted aloud another ubiqitous sign of the times: "There is no Planet B." And in that out-loud moment, it hit me how irrevocably we on Planet A are in this together.

**

An illustrative Duluth story: on our recent visit, unable to visit the delightful Tweed Museum of Art, shut down for renovations, I discovered Duluth's American Indian Community Housing Organization (AICHO). Closed because of COVID-19, AICHO's website offered what I was hungry to see: an online gallery of art created by Indigenous people of the Great Lakes. (As will be noted in these pages, at a previous visit, I'd become a huge fan of Rabbett Before Horses Strickland when visiting the Tweed Museum of Art.)

And lo, what did I discover? Another version of the Skywoman creation story that begins Robin Wall Kimmerer's *Braiding Sweetgrass*—a retelling which speaks to me. For in

Karen Savage Blue's lyrical depiction, Skywoman reaches down into the icy, creature-rich waters of Lake Superior. Skywoman rescues Muskrat! Don't you love it?

I do. And it's why I am now the proud owner of a giclée print of Savage Blue's watery, female-deity, love-infused depiction.

I love that a creation story can shift. Change. Evolve. I love being reminded that creation continues. Co-creation continues. To be reminded that our universe is a work in progress. And so are we. All of us. I love that inbreaking happens: "If, as I believe, the soul has its root in God, it should not be strange or amazing that fresh installments of life break in from beyond us and refresh us," the Quaker mystic, Rufus Jones, tells us. And, yes, I love how Savage Blue tilts Michaelangelo's lateral, "The Creation of Adam" moment ninety degrees. Downward. Into creatured fluidity.

Yet what urgency, what wonder, what poignancy in as-it-happens—in the now—Skywoman about to grab Muskrat; mud-bearing Muskrat sprinting toward her open hand. My bare hand touching a possibly infectious mailbox handle. A precious granddaughter and I inhale the same foul air. And why I've kept the many in-the-moment references to the pandemic in this book or added brackets.

Victorian Hair Wreath, Oliver House,
Yates County History Center, Penn Yan, New York
Photograph used with permission.

The Materials of Grief

> An apprenticeship with sorrow requires a hands-on encounter in which we are invited to work with the materials of grief, its leaden weight, and the particular demands of melancholy. We can feel it already, just in these few sentences, that this apprenticeship leads us below ground, into the hallway of shadows and forgotten ancestors. Here we find the scattered shards of unattended grief, the pieces of unwept loss, and the shavings of old wounds swept into the corner.
>
> *The Wild Edge of Sorrow: Rituals of Renewal and the Sacred Work of Grief*, Francis Weller[1]

Because of climate change, it now rains more in greater Boston. Whenever it rains, I slip on my leak-proof red boots, my L.L. Bean raincoat, grab my sturdy umbrella, and, while grudgingly grateful I can afford such good foul-weather gear, am again furious I have to wear it.

I am often angry. Anger has been my perennial, go-to, number-one negative emotion. As accessible as air, anger has fueled whatever creative project I've produced. Furious at some outrageous injustice, I've used my anger like crackling, long-burning, robust logs to sustain my work. If I ventured into that interiority Francis Weller so beautifully describes and stumbled upon those "scattered shards of unattended grief," more than likely I kicked them to the curb.

But as this global pandemic goes on and on, my lifelong propensity to kick and to mask my anger is changing—because it has to.

A story about change: after braving another nasty squall to walk to my yoga pre-class, I shed my wet gear, grabbed my props, and joined the other women seated on blue bolsters, ready to discuss whatever our gifted teacher, Annie Hoffman, prompted us to consider. A sutra. A poem. A conversation about growing old. A reading from one of yoga master B.K.S. Iyengar's books. That soggy Valentine's Day of 2020, just weeks before the shutdown, Annie asked us to pair up and take turns talking about all that we loved. Go!

I'm pretty good at nonlinear thinking so, beginning with "Myself," I rattled off a random, not-ranked list: My grandchildren. Rachmaninoff's Piano Concerto Number 3. Sitting on my backyard deck drinking coffee and writing in my journal. My husband. Swimming; swimming anywhere although kettle ponds, like Walden Pond, are my favorite. My four daughters. My step-children. And since I'd so recently noticed that, despite wind and rain and cold and my perennial anger at what's happening to our precious planet, I'd felt toasty-warm walking to class, I added, "And my excellent rain gear."

After my partner and I had both shared and reflected, Annie instructed, "Now, of all the things you listed, choose one."

I chose my umbrella. My pricey, black and red, reinforced so-it's-better-in-the-wind-than-the-cheap-umbrellas-I-usually-buy umbrella.

"Now, almost as if that one thing were on an altar or shrine, reflect on that one thing for three minutes," Annie said.

I am a Quaker, so I am also pretty comfortable with silent reflection. Seated on a blue bolster in Annie's studio, I remembered learning about the Northeast's now-rainier weather from Bill McKibben's *Eaarth: Making A Life on a Tough New Planet*. I thought about how, like McKibbens's altered spelling, I, too, am changing. Adapting. A lifelong Goodwill and consignment store shopper, I'd paid retail for my rain gear! Because I had to. And because I can afford it. In that three minutes, something about privilege came to me—certainly something about my easeful, blessed life. Something about mutability and adaption came, too. Something, too, perhaps, about radical acceptance?

"Okay," Annie said. "Now. Let that one thing go." And Mary Poppins-like without Mary Poppins, my sturdy umbrella floated up and into the rain-filled clouds.

"What is left?" asked Annie.

Me. That's what's left. I am left. Grateful me. Seventy-five-year-old me. The me who, like this tough, new Earth, must accept what is—and adapt, shift.

The me who, because both Annie and Marty Grundy, my spiritual advisor, urged me to read *The Wild Edge of Sorrow*, I dutifully read it.

And the me who—twice!—had recently blasted someone from my Quaker meeting—explosive outbursts, very public, very ugly.

"This is a pattern," I confessed to the three women in my Nurturing Faithfulness Group [Appendix B]. "All my life, I've masked my sorrow with anger. If I am to be faithful, maybe now is the time in my life when I am supposed to finally take an honest look at this—all of it. With your support. And with what comes through you." Weller's *The Wild Edge of Sorrow*, my workbook, my handbook—I underlined and scribbled in its margins and, gently guided by my group's questions, began my apprenticeship with sorrow.

A backstory about that fraught word, "apprenticeship": when my daughters were young and my parents joined us for Christmas, we'd read something aloud on Christmas Eve. My daughter, Christina, giggling as she read, loved the bit from *A Child's Christmas in Wales* when Miss Prothero asks the firemen if they'd like anything to read. And my father always chose the *Christmas Carol* scene set in Mr. Fezziwig's warehouse. It's Christmas Eve: urged to quit work by their boss, kindly, benevolent old Fezziwig, the adolescent Ebenezer Scrooge and his fellow apprentice, Dick Wilkins, quickly transform their boss's gloomy industrial space into a festive ballroom. In short order, the fiddler arrives to perform from old Fezziwigs's perched-above-the-warehouse desk. The Fezziwig family and neighbors and other warehouse employees troupe into the jollified room—spacious enough for twenty couples to dance. When the fiddler strikes up "Sir Roger de Coverly," Mr. and Mrs. Fezziwig, top couple, lead the way onto the dance floor. I can still hear his positive delight when Dad read, "A positive light appeared to issue from Fezziwig's calves."

Often an apprenticeship is cruel, dangerous, exploitative. I have come to associate this boss/fledgling worker relationship with old Fezziwig and a teenage Scrooge, however. A benevolent, generous, radiant—and genderless—Spirit guides me. Tenderhearted and grateful, I attend.

**

The same day in January when tens of thousands of Wuhan, China, residents attended a New Year's potluck, I attended a climate crisis gathering at my Quaker meeting. Over fifty people came. Seated in a gigantic circle in Friends Meeting at Cambridge's commodious Friends Room, one by one, we talked about why we'd shown up, what we grieved. Our collective sadness filled the room; our comingled grief and sorrow as real as the folding chairs we sat on or the paintings and wood cuts and wire sculptures hung on the Friends Room's walls, the ceramics exhibited in a glass case beside a window.

Allowing myself to let the feelings that filled that room fill me, something nudged: What would it be like to create something out of sadness? What material is sadness? Is it wire? Clay? Pastels on paper?

The next time our Nurturing Faithfulness Group met, I told them: "This apprenticeship is beginning to feel like a leading. I'm sensing I'm being asked to write about what I'm learning. But I'm still searching for a metaphor, an organizing principle, something to hold this whole whatever-it-is together." And I'd grinned. "But I know it'll come."

For, as my step-son, Jeremy, likes to say, "This is not my first rodeo." This is not my first leading. In 2000, I'd felt nudged to find the two Black teenagers who, in 1962, began classes at segregated E.C. Glass High School in Lynchburg,

Virginia—where I was a senior. My book, *Way Opens: A Spiritual Journey,* published in 2008, chronicles meeting and learning from Reverend Owen Cardwell Jr. and Dr. Lynda Woodruff.

I knew that if I were faithful to the promptings and nudges from Spirit, something would come. Something unexpected. Edgy, perhaps. Challenging? More than likely. But when this elusive metaphor showed up, I'd recognize it immediately.

In early March, two weeks before the pandemic shutdown, I had lunch at a Cambridge bistro with my dear friend and climate activist, Diana Lopez. How precious our in-person lunch together now seems! Surrounded by a noisy lunchtime crowd, squeezed together at a tiny table, we'd caught up over beer-battered fried fish tacos and lemonade. I'd briefly told her about my leading; she'd recently become fascinated by Elizabeth Cady Stanton. Perhaps sensing what COVID-19 was about to wreak, we'd speculated what it must have been like for Cady Stanton and her fellow suffragettes to have lived at a time of such enormous loss. That bloody Civil War, cholera, tuberculosis, children dying at alarming rates—such present, widespread loss and grief for those Victorians.

For Diana, having lost her beloved brother, David, six months before, loss and grief were not abstractions but present and real and sitting at that tiny table with us. Diana's palpable grief grounded our skittering conversation—despite the boisterous voices surrounding us.

Diana's sadness, imagining what it must have been like to live in the nineteenth century, my leading; suddenly I remembered a family visit to the Oliver House in Penn Yan, New York. Chockablock with ornate, fussy Victoriana, the museum had been near my parents' summer home. Toward the end of our self-guided tour, Dad pointed to a gilt and dark woodframed shadowbox on the wall. Something dark and worked and horseshoe-shaped had been preserved inside.

"It's a wreath made from hair," Dad explained. "People made these wreaths during Victorian times. It was how they remembered people they loved who had died."

In his tone, I'd heard disparagement; preternaturally cheerful, my father dismissed such silliness and sentimentality. Later, when I'd learned more about hair wreaths, I realized I'd also heard in my father's voice his dismissal of the handiwork created by women—mourning women.

"Yuck," my daughter Allison, age seven, pronounced. I'd felt a little queasy, too—yet, I remember, I had also found that wreath strangely and poignantly beautiful.

A hair wreath: what a perfect metaphor.

Here, then, is my handiwork, a circular hair wreath made from the strands of different hues and textures I've collected over the years. Some strands I've woven together, some are braided, some have been twisted into representational shapes and carefully placed around a sacred circle. Some of those shapes were made by my six grandchildren. Interspersed and intertwined, like the beads, shells, ribbons, or photographs those grieving Victorian women incorporated into their hairwreath handiwork, are photographs and musings and reflections on this extraordinary, unprecedented time we find ourselves in.

Pat and Al Wild on their wedding day, August 8, 1942, Bridgeport, Connecticut. Al, Pat, me, Paul, Deborah, Ben, our Ford Country Squire station wagon behind us, circa 1957, Fayetteville, New York. Background: A bubble-blowing family gathering for Mom's ninetieth birthday, Buzzards Bay, Massachusetts, April, 2013. (Mom is seated, center.)

Car Talk

When I think of my childhood, I see myself unseatbelted, untethered, and crammed into the "wayback" of a series of station wagons. On long trips, those station wagons' third seat would be removed; when it was my turn to occupy that squished space, I'd sit, facing backward, knees bent, on a mildewed Army-surplus sleeping bag next to my family's luggage. Sometimes on those long trips, Mom would open exactly one Wash 'n Dri moist towelette, which we'd pass along from the front seat to the back. By the time that singular piece of chemically treated paper got to me, that towelette would be desert-dry. And filthy. (How ridiculously liberating it had been when I became an adult and bought my own—and not to share!)

Once, I remember, in the rural South, the six of us crammed into a lime-green Dodge Polara station wagon, we'd stopped for gas on a hot summer afternoon, and my father bought himself a soda. I remember a mysteriously unrecognizable bottle, glass of course; it might have been emerald green, but that's probably wrong. Inches from my sipping father, hot, curious, thirsty, I stuck my head out of the back window to demand a sip. And still remember my astonishment to taste my first cream soda. *Cream soda.* Just whispering those three syllables still makes me happy.

Or that time on our Stow, Massachusetts, to Los Angeles road trip when I was eight, in our roomy, two-tone, green Dodge sedan, at twilight, soon after we'd crossed into California from Nevada. We'd stopped then, too, this time at a roadside stand, and my dad bought a date shake for all of us—five of us on that trip—to share. That had been the first time I experienced the dual pleasure of a new and delicious flavor, and bewilderment blended with admiration that my dad knew about exotic drinks.

Writing this as I begin my apprenticeship, so many questions: Why did the five of us sweating in that station wagon not get out, stretch our legs, catch a breeze, cool off under a tree? Why, on that sweltering day, had my father only bought himself something to drink? How did Al Wild, who'd never left New England until an adult, know about cream sodas and date shakes? Most peculiar, mysterious, telling: Where was Mom? Why isn't she in this story?

Tall, stunning, brilliant, no shrinking violet was our mom, Pat Wild. Not, in fact, the meek little wifeykins who twiddles her thumbs in a steamy car with four cranky kids, two of us teenagers, while her husband buys himself something cold and wet and delicious. Mom rarely held back. Married at nineteen to a polymath, charming, ambitious engineer eight years her senior, whose employment with the General Electric Company meant frequent moves, Pat Wild was often in the driver's seat. Because she had to be. Compelled to ferry her four children to piano lessons, to doctor appointments, to Cub Scout and Brownie meetings, to summer camp, and to the country club. If any of us failed to say, "Thanks for the ride,

Mom," within seconds of opening the car door, she'd tell us how ungrateful we were. (And often we were "thoughtless" and "heedless," too.) Like my father, Patricia Lillian Horrie Wild moved through the world as if she'd grown up wealthy; neither parent had. Her manners, like my father's, were impeccable. When it was time for her to hand over her car keys, ninety-something Mom had done so reluctantly—but with grace. As the staff at Neville Center, a long-term care facility in Cambridge, Massachusetts, had noted after she died, "Your mother was a classy lady."

My brother, Paul, two years younger than I, loved cars as a little boy. (Still does.) "Carth," he and I snicker now, recalling that beautiful, towheaded, blue-eyed little boy—who hadn't lisped but who did lie on his side on the living room floor of whatever house we lived in, his comely head resting on an outstretched arm, narrating elaborate stories featuring his favorite cars and trucks. Sometimes he made engine sounds as he pushed them around. On the road, year after year, he could identify the make and model of the traffic around us. (In those days, car design changed every year.)

Paul is pretty sure that the foundational childhood story I'm about to tell happened inside a baby-blue, cushy, and ample-spaced 1953 Buick Special with a white roof and, like all Specials that year, sporting three portholes on the side. (But it might have happened in the Dodge we would take to L.A.)

Siblings often remember childhood events differently, but on several details, Paul and I both agree: we'd been living in rural Stow, Massachusetts, fifty miles from Boston, in an eighteenth-century, salmon-colored colonial house with a neglected two-acre apple orchard behind the house, a robust lilac bush by the garage, and workable fireplaces—a necessity in rooms like my bedroom that had no other source of heat. We remember Debby hadn't been born yet; neither had Benjy. We remember that it had been raining that day. We remember the rhythmic windshield wipers, a gloomy afternoon, our lovely mother with her hands at nine and three on the steering wheel. We agree that we'd been standing on the backseat's floor, holding on to the cushy front seat's back and how, as we listened, we'd looked straight ahead. We watched the rain. We watched the windshield wipers.

"Mom?" one of us asked. "Dad tells us stories about his childhood all the time. How come you don't tell us about when you were a little girl?"

She equivocated; she hemmed and hawed; she claimed she couldn't remember. And then, giving in, here's what she told us:

> When I was a little girl, every winter my mother and my grandparents and my sister and I drove from Bridgeport, Connecticut, to Saint Petersburg, Florida, where we rented an apartment for a month. I went to school in Saint Petersburg. One year, on my last day, the teacher announced that I would be going back to Bridgeport the next day. I said goodbye, and then I left the classroom and closed the door behind me. But when I was just outside, I heard the whole class applaud and cheer! "Yay! She's gone!" The teacher told them to be quiet—but it was too late. I'd already heard them.

The way we remember it, Paul and I just stared at each other. And then burst into tears.

"What's the matter?" my mother wondered, genuinely puzzled it seems now. "Why are you crying?"

"That's a horrible story!" one of us had to explain to our mother. And we never asked about her childhood again.

Deborah, called "Debby" for most of her childhood, was born soon after that teary incident, and a couple of years later, Benjy, now Ben, completed our family—a few months after we'd moved from Stow to Fayetteville, New York, a suburb of Syracuse. Our larger family meant trading in that cushy Buick for our first station wagon, a Ford Country Squire with plastic siding molded to look like wood.

Another car story: again, it had been raining and, again, Mom had been driving. We'd just been to Syracuse where Debby, age three, had been fitted with her first glasses, and we were driving home. My multitalented sister—a gifted, consummate artist—sat in the front seat on Dad's lap.

"Look," glasses-wearing Debby crowed, transported, pointing to the streams of raindrops racing down the passenger-side window. The way I remember it, my father looked across at my mother; they'd exchanged horrified, oh-dear-God looks. And then my dad cried. Briefly and efficiently. Stone-faced, Mom kept driving.

Recalling this, again I wonder: Where was Mom? What was going on for her?

It's possible my father didn't cry and that I, granddaughter of Florence Mirick Wild, who always left a story better than she found it, have cinematically conflated the raindrops of the car window and my father's tears. It is also painfully possible that those remembered tears were my own, years later, when I realized, much too late, that my daughter, Christina, now an insightful, innovative teacher, much attuned to her students' needs, had also needed glasses.

A final car story: in the fall of maybe 1956 or 1957, seated side by side on that Ford station wagon's second seat and on our way from Fayetteville to Rochester, New York, Paul and I were again told something we would never forget. Paul had been nine or ten; I would have been eleven or twelve. This time our father drove, Mom beside him; Debby, maybe three or four, and Benjy, one or two, were left at home with a babysitter.

This just-the-four-of-us outing had been billed as a special lunch to be followed by a football game between Dad's alma mater, Tufts College, and the University of Rochester. Its real purpose became clear, however, as we exited the Thruway. Both of us remember driving down a highway ramp as our father announced: "Before we get to Rochester, there's something your mother and I want to tell you." We waited.

"As you know," Dad continued, "we've been very worried about Benjy—how weak he is. We've seen many doctors, and what we have heard is something we feel you're both old enough to know. Benjy may not live much longer."

Paul and I remember stunned silence; maybe we'd cried. We remember briskness, parental duty wafting from the front seat, a lofty scent of "There! Now You Know. We Have Done What We Feel Is Right" in the air. We remember the "There!" too-briskly becoming "Now, where should we eat?"

Those mid-century doctors misdiagnosed Ben. He is still with us and an altogether stellar human being, a retired career and technical education teacher, a superb woodworker, a loving husband, father of two wonderful adult children, and a doting grandfather.

But we station-wagoned four couldn't know that, any more than we could anticipate what it would mean to be that little boy's mother or father or sibling. We couldn't know how, sometimes, we'd remember Benjy's prognosis, but sometimes we'd get caught up in trumpet lessons, catching a plane, laundry, *Mickey Mouse Club*. We four couldn't know how sometimes we'd slow down, breathe, "smell the roses" first, ourselves, before cutting off a fragrant branch or two, removing the thorns, and handing this bouquet over to Benjy—how we'd sometimes savor life and find ways to share its beauty and joys with the youngest member of our family. We wouldn't know that, one hot summer afternoon when Benjy was three or four, we'd take him to a crowded petting zoo where he, completely attuned to a traumatized bunny, would crouch down to whisper to that frightened creature until it visibly relaxed. We couldn't know all we'd learn from him. Nor could we know that, to a large degree, the best part of who all four of us were to become—this would be true for Deborah, as well—was because of Ben.

What, in that stunned moment, could Paul and I have known? As bewildering as it seems to me now, our parents thought we should hear this devastating information. This *should* was entwined with a sense of duty, of responsibility, yes, but with something resembling integrity, too, I think. My mother and father deemed it morally right to entrust Paul and me with this news; like, and yet not at all like, Paul and I knowing there was no Santa Claus but keeping our superior knowledge a secret so that our little brother and sister could enjoy Christmas. (Even after Ben knew there was no Santa Claus, he kept his superior knowledge a secret for a year or two, fearing his enlightenment meant the end of Christmas for the Wilds.) For the general health and well-being of our family, Mom and Dad believed their two oldest children should know Ben's prognosis.

"They did the best they could," Paul and I now sum up.

And this key takeaway too: in our family, sadness is something you either don't do at all or do sparingly. Efficiently. There. Now you know. Where should we eat? "Don't wallow in it," we four were instructed.

So we didn't.

Here, then, is the skeletal wire frame for this materials-of-sadness hair wreath. The wreath may be too small or too large. It may be gangly, misshapen, lopsided. The wire is recycled—a rusty coil found in Dad's workbench drawer, perhaps. But this wire frame will hold this circular wreath together the best it can.

Mom in front of the
Cogill family tombstone,
Mountain Grove Cemetery,
Bridgeport, Connecticut.
[From a booklet I'd made
about our 2003, mother-
daughter Bridgeport trip.]

Forgotten Ancestors

In January of 2020, the same day Beijing reported its first COVID-19 death, out of the blue, I decided to rescue family photos mounted in moldy photo albums or crammed into shoeboxes under my bed. After buying a nifty storage box, I began to sort and organize. That same week, Ancestry.com informed me that my ancestors had been English, Scottish, Norwegian, and German. (I'd hoped to learn something startling.) A local historian contacted me, again out of the blue, to learn more about my great-grandmother, Amy, who had been a Faulkner before marrying Benjamin Franklin Wild. (He'd preferred "Frank.")

That synchronistic week continued: StoryCorps notified me that a family history story set in Somerville, which I'd recorded a few years earlier, was now accessible at the Library of Congress. I reconnected with my beloved second cousin, Peter Wild. And that Saturday, I'd been invited to visit a recently opened and beautifully organized food pantry in the roomy basement of the Mission Church of Our Lord Jesus Christ on Highland Avenue—just a few blocks from my house. From 1894 until 1975, Mission Church had been "First Unitarian

Somerville" and was located next door to Amy and Frank's mansion, now razed, where three generations of Wilds, including my father and my Aunt Amy, once worshipped.

That Sunday, still able to worship in person in the Friends Meeting at Cambridge's meetinghouse, I reflected on that week. What does all this family stuff in one week mean? Seated with a hundred or so fellow worshippers, we'd experienced a deep quiet for over half an hour before someone stood to break the silence. And in that long and delicious time to deepen and reflect, something came to me: "You call these random, all-the-same-week incidents family. Yet most of the happenstances this week have been about Wilds. Most of the photos in your nifty storage box are Wilds. You know next to nothing of your mother's history."

This accurate observation had been followed by a nudge: "And isn't it about time for you to find out?" Or, as I would come to view this Spirit-sourced prompt: "Here is the first exercise of your apprenticeship. Go!"

The next day, when I Googled for clues, I discovered that I hadn't known how to spell my maternal grandmother's maiden name—it's Cogill—and that I'd been spelling my maternal grandfather's first and last names wrong, too. My ignorance humbled me; to immediately realize how little I knew seemed a gift, an opening, an invitation to apply what Buddhists call "beginner's mind" to this apprenticeship: to be curious, open-hearted, eager. And stumbling upon the actual spelling of my grandfather's name had been "serendipitous," to use a word my mother often employed (sometimes incorrectly), and a reminder that, indeed, way opens.

My maternal grandparents divorced when my mother was a toddler; her father was never a part of her life. In 1966, however, when she and my father vacationed in Palm Beach, Florida, he had reentered her life. "You know, Al," she'd mused one night at dinner, "I think my father lives here." Low lights, flowers, a delicious, expensive seafood dinner, and a bourbon or two probably contributed to her pensive mood. Encouraged by Dad—"There's two sides to every story, Pat," he reminded Mom—she called her father who, I want to believe, immediately jumped in a cab to meet his daughter.

Did my grandfather stand for a few moments at the entrance to the dining room scanning the tables for Mom? Did his face light up when he spotted her—the stunning, middle-aged, well-dressed woman craning her elegant neck to scrutinize every man entering the room? When he'd approached my parents' table, had all three shook hands? Hugged? What were the first things my mother and her father said to each other? Had their initial conversation been stiff? Awkward? Warm? I don't know. As already noted, my mother wasn't much of a storyteller. I do know that, sometime during this reunion, Mom announced that I would be getting married that July.

"I'm coming," her father declared. In that declarative moment, did my mother remember all the times in her childhood when she'd longed for a proverbial dad? The dapper, elderly stranger who'd showed up—in spats—to my first wedding had been "Munro" not "Monroe." And his last name was "Horre." Not, as my mother, her sister Kay, and her mother spelled it, "Horrie."

I'd known—but forgotten—that "Horre" to "Horrie" spelling-change story, too; its broad outline, at least. When I'd been maybe ten or eleven, Mom explained, "My mother went to court. She added the "i." You'd think that with a name like Horre, she might have added a few more letters!" Too young and too cosseted, I didn't get Mom's joke. Twice-divorced, I can now also appreciate how my grandmother, who wanted to be called Lil and not Grandma, had inserted an "i" into her ex-husband's last name. I love how Lil inserted her personhood, her selfhood. I.

I remember that inserted-i story. But do I also remember a veiled look, how my lovely mother might have looked away, twirled a lock of her wavy brown hair or stared at her wedding ring when she'd finished telling it? Had she "cleaned her molars" with her tongue, as my sister and brothers called this Mom-tell which signaled, "I'm done! And angry. No more. Stop!"

The serendipitous story (and it really is): seven months and two days before the Wall Street Crash of 1929, Munro Horre and Muriel Kershaw applied for a marriage license and earned a tiny notice in *The Palm Beach Post*. I only discovered my grandfather's name misspelling because someone researching Kemp family history had apparently clipped a two-paragraph snippet—which had also included Munro and Muriel's announcement. And because of "a little thing I like to call 'the internet,'" as my daughter, Hope, says, there that snippet was, waiting for me to find it.

Although newspapers misspell names all the time, seeing my grandfather's name in print felt solid. Real. Important. I liked looking at this little scrap of information. So I took a screenshot of this small memento of the grandfather I met once but never knew and sent it to my four daughters and my sister.

Horre. Munro Horre. Who, during my mid-sixties-hippie-style-wedding-in-a-park reception, having just met his other daughter, my Aunt Kay, sidled up to my mother and whispered, "I like you more than her!" Munro Horre.

(Spellcheck keeps asking if I actually mean Horror. And maybe I do.)

Thanks to the internet, I located a Cogill family lineage tracing back to the mid-eighteen hundreds, too. I printed it out. I hole-punched it and reverently placed those family names and dates, as dry and as dusty as the "begats" of the Bible, in a three-ring binder. Thanks to the internet, I learned that Lillian Cogill Horrie died in 1961 at the horrifyingly young age of fifty-nine. (No wonder she hadn't wanted to be called "Grandma!")

Possessing a Cogill family lineage or doing simple arithmetic to learn that Lil had been forty-two when I'd been born didn't speak to my condition, however. This exercise had not been about left brain, three-ring binders, or pouring over census records. I was not supposed to research my mother's family's history.

What had I been gently nudged to do? To spend some time wandering through that metaphorical hallway of shadows and forgotten ancestors; that's what this exercise had been about. To inhabit that mournful word, "forgotten," but supply my own adjectives as well. Like lost. Unacknowledged. Denied. Stricken from the records. Missing. Never named. Gone. To walk past artist renderings of my English, Scottish, Norwegian, and German ancestors in that hallway of shadows and forgotten ancestors, to study the more recent portraits and photographs of the New Englanders listed in my three-ring binder, and, at last, to discover that where Munro Horre's portrait ought to be is an empty frame. To stand in front of that empty frame, its brass nameplate correctly spelled, to feel the sadness of his not-there-ness. To connect with my mother's sadness. And to begin to connect with my mother differently.

※※

My first apprenticeship exercise had been about connecting my own and my mother's sense of loss with humanity's collective loss—our shared grief. All our lost, missing, gone ancestors. All their lost wisdom. All the revelatory stories we will never hear. "When an old person dies, a library burns down," an African proverb reminds us. What enormous loss we all carry.

My sense of loss was to become enlarged, more painful, and more focused soon after that weirdly synchronistic week. Thanks to Ancestry.com, I learned that an eighth cousin—she and I share a common ancestor nine generations back—is a young woman of color. More than likely, our common ancestor had been male and white. More than likely, our shared DNA means rape, coercion, a violent sexual assault.

Horrified and devastated, I sought guidance from family and friends—and my apprenticeship handbook. And found this: "The cumulative grief of the world is overwhelming," Weller notes.[2] And he counsels us to hold this enormity in our hands, to cup our hands as if holding water in order to offer ourselves a bottom, a limit—to perform this ritual in order to contain all these powerful feelings.

Unaccustomed to ritual yet appreciative of how Weller's suggestion both acknowledged and honored what I was feeling while offering those feelings a safety net, I held that galactic grief. I embodied it. I honored it by lovingly cupping it in my hands. I grieved my own forgotten ancestors—and humanity's. I held in the Light my eighth cousin's forgotten ancestors, brought to this country in chains, whose real names and those of their descendants have been lost, forgotten, erased. I grieved those unnamed men and women and children who'd once walked on this tiny patch of Somerville real estate I call "mine." I grieved for my fatherless mother.

I held that. For a few terrifying moments, I allowed myself to experience momentous grief. But then, my left brain kicked in: "You can never adequately cup water in your hands. You can never hold it all." And I spread my fingers wide.

**

Lil died in 1961; my adored and cosmopolitan Aunt Kay, Kathryn Horrie Salwitz, died in 2006; Mom died in 2018. Were I living during the Victorian era, I might have saved strands of Lil's wiry gray hair, Kay's wispy blond, Mom's curly brown. I would have stored these handicraft materials in a pretty, enamel, covered bowl with a dime-sized hole in its cover, a hair receiver I kept on my bureau or dressing table. When my hair receiver was full, I might have created something wistfully beautiful from those strands. I might have incorporated something into whatever I crafted, a jet bead or two,[3] perhaps, to symbolize my yearning to know more of Lil's and Kay's and Mom's and, yes, Munro's stories.

My yearning is a tell, apparently. "Mostly, what the soul does is yearn," says David Brooks.[4]

"Grief work is soul work," Weller says.[5]

What does that even mean?

A kettle pond, still frozen, Mt. Misery,
Lincoln, Massachusetts, March 15, 2020.

Grief Work Is Soul Work

What is the soul?

Another car story; this one features my father—who'd been driving. In my mid-thirties by now, I'd sat in the middle seat of my parents' minivan, behind my father, and we'd been going—where? I don't remember. Somewhere in upstate New York's Finger Lakes region, though. For over a decade, my parents had a summer place we'd dubbed Big Pink in Prattsburgh, New York, with nine acres and a pond and, yes, a pink farmhouse. I see my parents and daughters only as silhouettes in that minivan, shoulder to shoulder, seatbelted, cruising up and down that region's soft, rolling hills past run-down Greek revival homes and vineyards and hardscrabble farmland along a two-lane, well-maintained state road, that summer afternoon's three-dimensional clouds above us.

Someone mentioned reincarnation, and my father pooh-poohed. "People want to believe in reincarnation because it's convenient," he scoffed. "No one knows what happens after we die. But people need to believe in something."

"But, Dad," I argued to the back of his head, "how can you accept a universe that doesn't recycle something as precious as a soul?"

Without planning to, without really understanding what I was talking about, I had scored an Al Wild double whammy.

Blow one: my father's take on religion was a shoulder-shrugging, "I can take it or leave it," but he definitely worshipped efficiency—the Gilbreths of *Cheaper by the Dozen* fame were household gods[6]—and who no doubt believed God to be male and a fellow engineer. (Although I do remember him questioning some of the Creator's decisions: "Why are there so many different birds," he puzzled. "Why do they have so many different colors? I can't understand that.") Ever the engineer, even when telling one of his long-winded and mostly wonderful stories, he'd often stop his narrative to excitedly describe some random, ingenious machine or gadget lurking in his story's background until, much to the relief of his impatient listeners, finally getting back to the storyline.

Blow two: my dad had been a frugal Yankee. Not as in the baseball team but as in what people who'd grown up in New England are sometimes called. As in *Yankee Magazine*. People who eat peas and salmon on the Fourth of July and root for the Red Sox—even when there's no hope. People who'd recycled long before the rest of us believed recycling would save the world.

"Well," my frugal, thoughtful father replied, "you make an interesting point."

I don't kid myself that, because of something I'd said, my father immediately and forever changed his mind about reincarnation. The takeaway from that car story is that I, warmed and supported by Dad's respectful listening, became even more curious about this vaguely understood soul I'd just referenced.

Soul food, *Soul Train*, good for my soul—of course I'd heard the word, but what did I actually know about my own soul? I certainly don't remember any discussion on the topic in my Unitarian Universalist Sunday School classes. Pretty sure that, although I'd received an excellent religious education, the UU's Beacon Press didn't offer books on the subject. *Beginnings of Earth and Sky,* yes. *Child of the Sun: A Pharaoh of Egypt,* yes. *Men of Prophetic Fire,* yes. *Jesus the Carpenter's Son,* yes. *The Church Across the Street,* yes. (This last book, about a baker's dozen of American religions, omitted Islam but included the Society of Friends. Its compelling description contributed to my becoming a Quaker.)

A little personal history sleuthing revealed how this soul-curiosity began. One Christmas, when I was maybe eight, I received Bullfinch's *Age of Fable.* Studying my yellowed and slightly mildewed copy now, its black-and-white ink drawing of Psyche, a lamp in her left hand, a knife in her right, as she beholds a graphically naked, curiously beautiful Cupid with folded wings, might be why I'd read that particular myth first. And continued to read and reread that story because—well, Psyche and Cupid! Such a great story, right?

In the nineties, when teaching in Boston-area shelters, I retold this childhood favorite to a young, unhoused mother who'd wanted to become a psychologist—and was understandably annoyed by her chosen profession's spelling. So I'd explained to her how Freud, by referencing this myth, was saying that humans can be both human and, like Psyche, transformed.

"Good story," she'd declared.

"Psyche, then, is the human soul, which is purified by sufferings and misfortunes and is thus prepared for the enjoyment of true and pure happiness," Bullfinch concludes.[7]

Over time, other sources have instructed me about my soul. Over thirty years ago, for example, when my second marriage ended, I read Thomas Moore's *Care of the Soul* as avidly as another devastated person might read the Psalms. Now, thumbing through my underlined and battered paperback—apparently I'd read that book while soaking in the bathtub more than once—to reread what I'd noted in purple ink thirty years ago is touchingly similar to rereading my journal from that painful time.

Things like this: "Jealousy is the preservation of the hearth and interiority. If we did not become jealous, too many events would take place, too much life would be lived, too many connections made without deepening. Jealousy serves the soul by pressing for limits and reflection." "Reflection" had been circled with purple ink.[8]

Why this statement spoke to me could be the central theme of another memoir. What moves me now, however, is that purple-circled word, *reflection*. Which means, I think, that, although in deep pain, I'd realized I'd needed to ponder (to borrow a word my daughter, Allison, loved as a child). To assess. To question. To be honest with myself.

And I did. And, perhaps for the first time in my life, I honestly acknowledged my outsized anger. Held by Eric Beutner, a dear friend I'd known from my earliest days at FMC, I sobbed every Sunday morning during meeting for worship—until I didn't. Until I was cried out. Until I found a therapist. Until, while soaking in the bathtub, I read the self-help books my friends suggested. Or while devouring bags of Chips Ahoy.

Another bit from Moore before moving on:

> The ultimate work, then, is an engagement with soul, responding to the demands of fate

and tending the details of life as it presents itself. We may get to a point where our external labors and the opus of the soul are one and the same, inseparable. Then the satisfactions of our work will be deep and long lasting, undone neither by failures nor flashes of success.⁹

Ten years after I'd underlined Moore's words, my first writing-as-my-ministry book, *Swimming in It,* based on the stories my unhoused students told me, was published. (At a fictionalized Quaker memorial for one of my novel's main characters, the real young woman who'd wanted to become a psychologist makes a cameo appearance. With heavy, dramatic eye makeup.) And here I am, dear reader, writing this opus of the soul. Still writing.

Like my quarantined friends who finished that sweater they'd started three years ago or learned how to bake bread or played music with their neighbors, as an assignment for my apprenticeship, I decoded a book I'd heard referenced many times but never read, Rufus Jones's *The Testimony of the Soul.* A Quaker mystic, Jones wrote this sometimes-opaque opus during the Great Depression. And while I found Jones's references to his fraught time both moving and applicable to this fraught time, slogging through his *Testimony* was slow going. Highly motivated, however, my schedule suddenly radically freed up, I took whatever time I needed to comprehend, word by word, paragraph by paragraph, and, lo, the Red Sea parted!

Here's a wonderful, mixed-metaphor sample from that book:

> There is an interior depth-life in man that carries rich veins of wealth which should be

> carefully assayed. The historical trails to the headwaters of our faith are being profoundly searched today and those historical researches are accumulating stores of spiritual riches. We need not tremble for the preservation of the truth which History enshrines. It will not be lost.[10]

And another sample: "If, as I believe, the soul has its root in God, it should not be strange or amazing that fresh installments of life break in from beyond us and refresh us."[11]

Perhaps it's not surprising that, since my beloved father had been such a pivotal, significant influence in my life, I'd seek out the writings of wise and insightful men like Jones and Moore and Weller to understand what "soul" means. So while a little sheepish about my wonky need to do my homework, I am nevertheless grateful for Jones and Weller, *et al.*, whose writings have been foundational to this apprenticeship.

However, like so many eye-rolling moments with my Republican, stodgy father, especially during the Vietnam War, I have been sometimes brought up short by something I have read. No matter how zealously I tried to "read in tongues," for example, Jones's almost-exclusive use of the male pronoun got in my way.

And sometimes, during this reading period, wise as these men were, what I read did not speak to my condition. I strongly disagree with Bullfinch's conclusion that we must suffer in order for our soul to be purified, for example. Like many before me have believed, I hold that our soul does not require purification by pain or suffering to keep on keepin' on. We are born with a soul, I believe—a purified soul. It's standard equipment. No add-ons or upgrades or special apps required.

We see it every time we look into a baby's eyes. Like that lovingly documented "Patty," the toddler whose black-and-white pictures fill a couple of those plastic boxes in my nifty attaché case, my soul has stumbled and fallen yet unerringly gravitated toward what it craves. Yearns for. For most of my blessed life, I have learned experientially what fills me; I have sensed, without words, what I need:

Music. Beauty. Love. My family. Being in nature. Being in community. Being in communion with Spirit. Prayer. Silence. Intentional, protected time to reflect, noodle, idly watch contrails from my backyard hammock while serenaded by the neighborhood mockingbird. Or, as I'd once done every summer, to lie on a float in the middle of my parents' pond to watch those puffy, three-dimensional clouds move overhead. And as this apprenticeship is making clear, I need ritual as well.

Does this list sound vaguely familiar?

Yes, as that purple-circled "reflection" reminds me, pain and suffering and terrible moments in our lives ask us to make meaning—to ponder, to seek, to look at ourselves with razor-sharp acuity, and to draw on something within ourselves to find our way through. And if, like Psyche, we can emerge from the depths of those infernal shades, in the fullness of time, we may look back at those searing experiences with something like gratitude.

I did. I have emerged from hard times. I have experienced such gratitude—and continue to. But there are many people, some of them my dear friends, who have not. Cannot.

**

Sometimes we're blessed. Spirit inbreaks—to echo Jones, but employ a verb often used by my spiritual advisor, Marty Grundy, whose pronouns are she/her/hers. Sometimes we gratefully call these inbreaking moments "grace." Sometimes, I've come to realize recently, these transcendent, fresh installment, soul-touched moments can be understood as mystical experiences.

I'd had such a mystical experience during that painful period in my life—while on my way to teach at a homeless shelter. What I most remember of that inbreaking—besides my indescribable joy—is how out of the blue it seemed. And how inconvenient!

Driving down Massachusetts Avenue through Porter Square during morning rush hour, I'd half-listened to *Morning Pro Musica* on WGBH when Fauré's "Messe Basse" began. Three or four measures into this exquisite, women-sung piece, I suddenly experienced Spirit's piercing, all-embracing love for me, for everyone, for the life surrounding me.

"But why now?" I puzzled. "On my way to work? Why couldn't this Light-filled moment happen in a forest or on a beach—so I could actually savor it?"

So I'd welcomed the red light at the intersection of Massachusetts and Somerville Avenues to more fully listen. The first movement, "Kyrie eleison," ended, the organist held a chord for a few beats, and then the soprano soloist began "Sanctus"; almost immediately, other sopranos and altos joined in. From the ever-so-slight echo of their *dolce* voices, I easily imagined a Gothic church with stone walls, imposing pillars, stained glass, beeswax candles.

The music continued, "Hosannah in excelsis." While harried pedestrians streamed toward the T entrance, I glanced to my left, to the Porter Square Shopping Center's already full parking lot and the concrete wall abutting the Mass Ave sidewalk. There, as always, sat ten or fifteen "wall people," as my unhoused students called them, Somerville and Cambridge unhoused people, many holding coffee containers from the nearby Dunkin' Donuts. (There is always a nearby Dunkies in greater Boston.) Like always, the wall people sat, sipped, smoked, argued. And I, imbued by Love and its attendant sense of profound connection with all, realized that the only possible difference between the wall people and me was that they had not yet felt what I was feeling. Not yet.

When that musical jewel ended, *Morning Pro Musica*'s host, Robert J. Lurtsema, another greater Boston institution, identified the piece as Fauré's "Low Mass." After work that day, I walked to Harvard Square to buy my own CD. And for years I assumed I'd experienced that wondrous, all-loving moment largely because of what Robert J. chose to play that morning.

But one Sunday morning during the shutdown, at a Zoom meeting for worship, a member of my meeting, Dinah Starr, told the story of how Thomas Merton experienced an eerily similar moment. Dinah later sent me the text from the Trappist monk's book, *Conjectures of a Guilty Bystander*:

> In Louisville, at the corner of Fourth and Walnut, in the center of the shopping district, I was suddenly overwhelmed with the realization that I loved all these people, that they were mine and I theirs, that we could not be alien to one another even though we were total strangers. It was like waking from a dream of separateness, of spurious self-isolation in a special world.

> Then it was as if I suddenly saw the secret beauty of their hearts, the depths of their hearts where neither sin nor desire nor self-knowledge can reach, the core of their reality, the person that each one is in God's eyes. If only they could all see themselves as they really are. If only we could see each other that way all the time. There would be no more war, no more hatred, no more cruelty, no more greed. . . . But this cannot be seen, only believed and "understood" by a peculiar gift.[12]

Inbreaking happens. Mystical moments happen. No soundtrack required.

**

What twisted or braided-strand shape or shapes should grace that good-enough wire frame? Two or three butterflies, I think, of varying sizes. Long associated with Psyche, transformation, and beauty, in recent years, the butterfly has come to symbolize the immigration rights movement's yearning for justice. That a butterfly's delicate, winged stage is that transformational creature's final state reminds me of how ephemeral, how brief these soul-touched moments can be. And that I, too, am in my final state.

A beheaded but inspirational Alice Neel self-portrait lurks in the background.

Like Something out of Dickens

When I think of my mother's childhood, I think of her reading. I want to think of her happily engrossed in a favorite book to escape her wretched childhood, a childhood "like something out of Dickens," as I'd explained to a series of therapists when ready to examine my relationship with my mother. I don't want to remember that reviled little girl outside a raucous St. Petersburg classroom. I chose to think of her living with her mother and sister in her grandparents' elegant Bridgeport, Connecticut, home and cozily settled in an armchair near the living room fireplace; I see her reading and rereading her favorites while twirling her hair at the nape of her lovely neck—a lifelong habit.

I don't want to remember the little girl who, one night, lying in bed, heard her mother's brother, Franklin Cogill, her beloved uncle, cry out, "I don't want to die!" I don't want to think about that Pat Horrie, who'd been fourteen when Franklin, the most important, the most loving and supportive man in her life, died from tuberculosis of the kidney.

A handsome man who "swam like a dream," according to Mom, Uncle had been a champion swimmer at Yale, graduating with a civil engineering degree. Before returning home to die at his parents' home on 419 Mill Hill Avenue, now razed, he'd been a salesman for Ingersoll-Rand. Uncle came home on weekends—when he'd often helped my mother with her homework.

An Uncle story: evenings, Uncle liked to listen to a Bridgeport quiz show on the radio; to surprise him, one evening, Mom took the bus downtown to compete herself. (Like older women of that mid-thirties era, when she went downtown, Mom wore a hat with a veil. A straw hat, I'm guessing, dyed navy blue or black—which teenage Mom wore with her saddle shoes and bobby socks!) As a contestant, she'd done pretty well at first, doing herself and her teacherly uncle proud. A question about a figurative chain, its individual links able to withstand different pressures, stumped her, however. At what pressure would the chain break, Mom was asked. Believing that the link's individual strengths somehow combined and that Uncle had probably taught this formula to her, she'd panicked. Why couldn't she remember that formula?

"Remember, Pat," Uncle later told her. "A chain is as strong as its weakest link." By her weighty tone telling this story, Mom made clear that Uncle's metaphorical lesson had not been lost on her.

How do I, who spent most of my life knowing next to nothing about my mother, know these poignant details? Because in late October of 2003, when Mom had been eighty and I fifty-nine, she and I drove from her home on Cape Cod to Bridgeport. This two-day trip was to be my first opportunity to fill in some serious blanks in Mom's history. For surely there had been more to tell? I'd been moved to wonder. Surely Mom possessed more stories than *In Which Mom Had Been a Hated*

Classmate or, as my sibs and I would later hear, *In Which Mom Hears Her Dying Uncle Cry Out in Fear*?

I'd like to believe that, given Paul's and my unexpected tears that rainy day long ago, Mom held off sharing her Uncle story until all four of us were adults. And until after she'd begun to work full time and had instituted her "Thank God It's Friday" routine. Chips n' dip and bourbon over ice consumed, Mom would launch into phase two of this TGIF ritual: "I never told this story before, but—"

Five years younger now than Mom had been on that Bridgeport trip, I know more about trauma than I did on those tipsy Friday nights forty years ago. Not a trained psychologist, I have nevertheless observed that when people recount painful stories, they sometimes switch to present-tense verbs as if reliving that traumatic experience. They share these stories as though what happened is unfolding before their eyes. Now I can accept that, when my mother stated, "I never told this story before," her wide-eyed intro felt true for her.

I did not understand this back then. What I knew was that, on Friday nights, my mother kicked back, drank too much, and then told her horrible Uncle story again. Or the one about the man from the Huntsville (Alabama) Unitarian Universalist church who'd made a pass at her. I knew, when she began her preamble, how to inwardly roll my eyes and indignantly mutter, "Yeah, right," under my breath at her obvious lie. I also knew my mother would eventually toddle off to bed so, during the era when my parents had owned Big Pink, I would count off the minutes until I could go outside and smoke a joint. I believed that getting high was better than getting wasted. And I believed that an appropriate response to pathos was snickering, impatience, anger.

Or, as my father modeled: opportunism. Where was Dad in these stories? He'd waited, too. Offstage. His weight a struggle his whole life—until his first heart attack—and his "Al, you've had enough!" Calorie Cop indisposed, Dad fixed himself something prohibitively fattening for dinner; he puttered in the basement, the garage, in the barn. And when Mom finally exited, he would return to the living room and his favorite chair, to his pipe and a crisp new issue of *The Atlantic Monthly*, the local public radio's classical music program turned down low. He returned for a quiet evening. Alone.

A denouement to these told-when-in-her-cups stories: after Mom began therapy, she examined the Uncle story more deeply, adding, "And no one came to my bedroom to comfort me." Much later, after Mom and I had established a closer and deeper relationship, she again amended this painful story. "You would have, Patricia," she told me one Friday night. "You would have come to check on me."

Which might be the most wonderful thing my mother ever said to me.

How do I now, after all those years of anger and inurement, how do I access any of what was painfully true for my mother? What ritual will allow me to genuinely and reverently feel what my mother deserved: my compassion and, ah, there it is, my sadness, which, like Weller's image, has again been swept into the corner? What might illuminate that corner?

Had I yearned for a flashlight to search that neglected corner when I invited her to go with me to Bridgeport? Had I longed to hear other stories from my mother's past? I think I did. That trip, I think, had been soul work.

Reading my account of those two days, two moments shine some light, allowing me to see that corner and to access other feelings beside impatience—or anguish. One moment I only now can see for what it actually must have meant, one I'd witnessed but failed to record.

That now-more-deeply-understood moment happened when Mom and I drove to Walnut Beach in Milford, Connecticut, where her grandparents owned a beach house, Seagull, later destroyed in the 1938 hurricane. It was an empty lot now, but Mom had no trouble identifying the site by its location in relation to Charles Island, just off shore in Long Island Sound.

Charles Island had come up in a previous conversation that trip; here's what I'd recorded:

> Finding words to express what she was experiencing was sometimes difficult. "Thinness" was as close as Mom could get. "There was a thinness of imagination and curiosity in my childhood," she managed. "No adult ever took me to Charles Island," she said by way of example. Charles Island, located perhaps a half-mile from her family's summer home, was connected to the mainland by a sandbar visible at low tide.

Standing on the shoreline at Walnut Beach, Mom identified Charles Island; as if she thought I'd always known this, Mom then pointed to the Horre family's summer place—just a couple houses away from Seagull.

Misspelling my grandfather's name, here's how I recorded this moment:

> That's how Lil and Monroe Horrie first met: a summer romance. Seeing how close together these houses [had been] made me sad: "Did your father ever come here?" I asked Mom.
>
> "No," she said.

"Didn't you miss him?" I asked, remembering that little girl who longed for someone to walk with her to Charles Island.

"No," she responded, surprised.

But she did. She had.

How do I know this? Longing to learn what that bright and neglected child loved and took to heart unearthed a long-hidden memory: when I'd been ten or eleven, Mom and Dad had gone to see the movie *Daddy Long Legs*, released in 1955, starring Leslie Caron and Fred Astaire. Despite the movie's endearing, dancing stars, Mom had been disappointed. "The book was so much better," she'd complained the next day. "I'd loved that book as a child. I read it over and over."

The hyphenated-titled *Daddy-Long-Legs*, first published in 1912 and wildly popular for decades, was written by Jean Webster, a feminist and Vassar graduate, who'd drawn on her own collegiate experience when writing her book. Reading this charming YA classic nearly a century after Mom, I understood why this epistolary book had been a bestseller—and why my fatherless mother read it again and again.

Jerusha Abbott, an orphan as plucky and delightful as Anne Shirley of *Anne of Green Gables*, is a dogsbody at a cold and sterile orphanage. Immediately following her high school graduation ceremony, Jerusha is informed that one of the orphanage's trustees, who wishes to remain anonymous, is sending her to an all-women college, all expenses paid. Having made these generous arrangements, Jerusha's benefactor is just leaving the orphanage when the plucky orphan briefly catches sight of a tall, older man, or, rather, his elongated shadow: *Daddy-Long-Legs*. Required to write a monthly letter to this kindly, spindly phantom, Jerusha fills his mailbox with delightful, honest, and detailed accounts of college life, adding badly drawn, hilarious drawings sometimes, too.

Picturing my uncle-bereft mother, living in a home as arid as that fictional orphanage and reading and rereading that book broke my heart. Especially since, over and over, Jerusha pens how much she longs to meet her benefactor, how she wants to connect with Daddy-Long-Legs face-to-face, how often she begs him to show up. How could Pat Horrie *not* have identified with Jerusha? Of course she had!

Painful, too, is knowing that my brilliant mother, as hungry to learn and as curious as Jerusha, had read this lively novel about a young woman's college experiences—yet had felt obligated, in the middle of the Great Depression, to attend a one-year dental hygiene program because she didn't want to financially burden her family. So, I realized sadly, after reading Jerusha's animated accounts of campus life, my hungry and brilliant mother had known exactly what she'd missed out on.

Upon graduation from Columbia Dental Hygiene School in New York City, Mom returned to Bridgeport to clean its city's school children's teeth before, at nineteen, meeting and marrying my father. And then, like her Seven Sisters-educated neighbors and friends, Mom assumed the same enervating wife and mother and competent volunteer roles of the forties and fifties. No wonder the mother I remember from my childhood began so many sentences with "I never—" or "I wish I'd—" or "I've always regretted that I—"

Knowing what my mother had known about Jerusha's excitement to attend intellectually stimulating classes enlarges and amplifies a mom memory as sweet and rich as a slice of Virginia chess pie: in 1959, because my father's employer, the General Electric Company, transferred us and five-hundred other families from the Syracuse, New York, area to Lynchburg, Virginia, our family found ourselves living near Randolph Macon Woman's College—as it was then called. (Begun in 1893, RMWC became coeducational and renamed Randolph College in 2007.) Its gracious, brick-wall-encircled campus, as imposing and charming and artfully landscaped as Vassar's, Mom briefly yet joyfully claimed RMWC for her own, taking one, maybe two classes—theology classes, as I recall. Struggling to fulfill the classwork required by a full day of high school, I'd been silently dismissive of Mom's light load.

What warms me now is to remember how earnest she'd been, how dedicated, how happy. I'm also reminded of how resilient my mother had been throughout her life. How adaptable. How, like taking those enriching classes while living in an alien community, she'd carved out a way to take care of herself.

When I'd ordered my Looking Glass Library Edition[13] of *Daddy-Long-Legs* from Alibris, I did it because I'd wanted to own a book my mother had read and loved. But like that nifty, virtual umbrella I'd placed on a virtual altar and silently contemplated at yoga class, to place this purple-bound 2015 edition beside me as I write this has become a new ritual for me. Every time I look at it, I remember the deep sadness that welled up when, in one sitting, I read my mother's beloved book. To powerfully connect with the young girl who'd held a much earlier edition in her hands and turned its pages while twirling her hair? What a gift!

My copy of *Daddy-Long-Legs* beside me now, I wonder if, at that moment on Walnut Beach when Mom told me, no, she didn't miss her father, had I felt the briefest of nudges, like a soft ocean breeze against my cheek, an inward, "Huh?" Had that moment invoked another, "Yeah, right?" Had I searched her face to ascertain: can this possibly be true? Did I sense I'd asked my mother about a feeling she'd never experienced? Did I therefore decide, why bother, there's no reason to pursue this? Or had it been simply more convenient to accept at face value what she'd told me.

Related to my silence: in plain sight in another corner, no flashlight needed, is something I have stubbornly refused to acknowledge and, unacknowledged and denied, this something has accrued enormous power from the energy I've expended for seventy-five years pretending it's not there. Even though I've always been able to see it. Even though, from birth, I've always known it was there. My father adored me. The feeling was mutual.

Not surprisingly, then, how difficult it must have been, sometimes, for my fatherless, uncle-bereft mother to witness that love! And I have always known this. So her denial that day on the beach might have been a couple of steps of the dip-and-swing dance around her jealousy and pain my mother and I always danced, as if to say, "Hello, here it is, again; they're playing a salty, seagull-accompanied version of our song, Mom."

The second, revelatory moment happened the following day at the Cogill family plot in Bridgeport's Mountain Grove Cemetery, reportedly designed in 1849 by P.T. Barnum, one of the city's most notorious citizens, who is also buried there. (Barnum being Barnum, I suspect he'd hired a professional landscape designer but took all the credit for himself.) To spare my mother, I chose not to record what I'd observed, but I still remember it.

Surrounded by the cemetery's unraked yellow and crimson leaves, seemingly alone in that vast, park-like cemetery, I watched as Mom, seated on a little camp chair in front of the Cogill headstone, copied down family names and dates engraved in stone: "Papa," Frank Leander Cogill, her grandfather, a self-made, successful businessman whose nervous breakdown and years of pacing back and forth in the home he'd designed—and where Mom grew up—and subsequent hospitalizations in a Connecticut sanitarium wrote several grim chapters of my mother's Dickensesque childhood. Her grandmother, "Nana," also a Lillian. Her beloved "Uncle," Franklin. Her mother's sister, Arline, who'd died of typhoid at age nine. Her "Auntie Pearl" and Pearl's husband, Stuart Naramore; Mom recorded her inscribed family history.

But suddenly looked up, surprised: "My mother was just one year older than Franklin," she announced.

And as I watched her, I saw sudden realization cross her face. Because she knew what a brother's death, a brother so close in age to her mother, must have meant. Although not close to her own sister, she'd known siblings close in age and close to each other. She'd known Paul and me, watched the two of us grow up together; she'd observed loving-kindness between a brother and a sister. She had history; she had data; she had lived experience. She could understand Lil's love for Franklin, her dying brother. In that moment, seated on her camp chair, my mother newly understood her mother's deep loss and sorrow. Did it occur to her why Lil might not have had the strength or the energy to comfort her daughter when her beloved, dying brother called out?

I can still see all of those feelings and sympathies and deeply felt understandings cross my mother's face, an entire story told eloquently but without words. And how, willy-nilly, that story abruptly ended. She'd shut down, her lined yet still lovely face a blank, her blue eyes stolid. "I'm done. Enough. No more."

A metaphor from my childhood comes to mind: by the time she'd become a grandmother, Lil lived on the first floor of a sturdy, two-family house built in the twenties and located near Bridgeport Hospital, with stained glass windows in the dining room, a clawfoot bathtub, World War II blackout shades still on the windows, and thick, oak sliding doors between the living room and dining room. A sooty, grubby city back then, even if there had been a swingset in Lil's back yard or a playground nearby, being outdoors in Bridgeport in the early fifties wasn't fun.

So Paul and I improvised. Those sliding doors between the dining room and living room became elevator doors, he in the dining room, me in the living room. Or vice versa. Who played Passenger, who played Elevator Operator was fluid, too, because being the Passenger was about as much fun as being outside. Your role was to meekly give a floor number and then step inside. No, the real joy was to be the Elevator Operator who emphatically slammed those heavy doors shut. "Watch your fingers," you got to say. Then Slam! Whomp! At any moment, though, meek Passenger might suddenly choose to command the far more satisfying role of Elevator Operator and, willy-nilly, those satisfying, solid pieces of planed, paneled, shellacked wood would crash together again. And again—until some adult appeared to demand we knock it off, go outside, and play.

Whomp! So many complex reasons why Mom slammed shut!

**

Another baby blue Buick story: when I was ten, I'd gone to Camp Four Winds, a Girl Scout camp in Plymouth, Massachusetts. Those two disorienting weeks in August, my first extended time away from home, I'd been homesick, anxious, logy from swimming. (Besides an incipient ear infection, I'd also acquired a new identity: my cabinmates dubbed me "Pepper," a sobriquet I retained until I was thirty and finally ready to "put away childish things.")

Every night before falling asleep, my cabinmates chattering around me, I'd read. Why I borrowed that particular mildewed, battered, no-illustrations hardcover from the camp's carelessly shelved collection in its main hall is a mystery. So is its title. Googling "children's book" and "boy" and "barge" and "houseboat" and "river" and "lumber"—fresh-cut, sweet-smelling lumber, as I recall—offers no clues. As I read, I imagined I heard the soft, rhythmic sound of river water lapping against a fat-bellied barge, a lulling sound I knew well from vacations aboard sailboats. Lying in my sleeping bag on the bottom bunk of a no-frills, wooden cabin in Plymouth, Massachusetts, I'd been gently rocked to sleep.

When camp was over, two worth-noting things happened on the drive home to Stow: first, I'd learned we were to move again, this time to Syracuse, New York. (We'd end up in Fayetteville, south of Syracuse.) "Oh, good," I'd realized immediately, "I can tell people my name is Pepper, and they won't know any better." And second, I'd told my family—there were five of us that summer—about the boy-on-a-barge book. I remember my mother saying, "I read that book when I was your age! I'd loved it."

And for a moment, a mysterious, surprising, and miraculous moment, I conflated my previous two weeks of loneliness and confusion and the dull, throbbing pain of a chronic ear infection with my mother's melancholy childhood.

So much of my imagined wreath will be comprised of my mother's absently twirled hair!

Deepening

We'd just left Medford and another Sunday dinner at my paternal grandparents' snug house on Badger Road. Like always, Grandma had made lamb stew that she'd served in flowered, blue-rimmed bowls; the gamey, tough chunks of meat swaddled in fat swam in a greasy but strangely watery stew of overcooked but under-seasoned potatoes and carrots and celery. Under my grandparents' dining room's too-bright chandelier, straddling a *Boston Metropolitan Area Yellow Pages*, I'd swallowed three or four slithery mouthfuls, washed down with milk when no one was looking, because I knew that if I didn't significantly lower the amount of stew in my impossibly large bowl, I wouldn't get dessert. And Grandma excelled at desserts—pies, especially. Cherry or apple.

Headed back to Stow, Paul and I sprawled on the back seat, it was dark, nighttime. I remember a crescent moon. Traveling west on Route 2, watching the moon travel alongside our Dodge sedan, I suddenly realized that, since I was older than Paul—he'd needed to sit on two phone books at dinner—I would probably die before him! Immediately, I verified this likelihood with my parents—who'd reluctantly agreed from the front seat that, yes, probably what I'd speculated might happen.

Just thinking about all the wonderful and exciting things he'd get to do and experience and taste, lamb stew not being one, while I lay dead in my grave, I burst into tears. Such exclusion! So unfair! To this day, I still feel Paul's satisfied gloating; I know he'd been grinning in the dark.

At five or six, I must have imagined death to be like being punished and sent to bed without supper. While I lay in bed, my bedroom windows open, my brother would be outside, free, right under my window, shrieking with pleasure. Maybe he'd been given a second slice of Grandma's cherry pie. While I, empty stomach rumbling, lay in bed and heard his delight, my pillow wet from jealous, silent sobbing.

Silent sobbing, yet immobile. For although I'd whined about a classic childhood travesty, "How come he gets to . . . and I don't?" when I'd sobbed in the backseat of that car, I'd mourned myself. My own death. I'd felt it; I'd recognized death's stone-cold irrevocability. Which I knew a little about. A couple of years before, I'd inadvertently killed a caterpillar when I'd given one a bath—and had even thoughtfully provided its curved, fuzzy, inert body with a tiny tent, made from an opened book of matches, to dry beneath—so at five, I already knew that dead things don't move.

From the front seat, my Route 2 tears were dismissed, as my own and my siblings' childhood tears were often dismissed, as the by-product of a long day. "It's been a long day. It's late," our parents would counsel. "Time for bed. (Or a nap.) You'll feel different in the morning."

What had prompted this intimation of mortality? A grandmother myself, I wonder if all grandchildren don't look at their grandparents with a sense of foreboding. Vain child that I was, I certainly did. I'd stare at Lil's wattled, double chin, her crepey neck so yellow-white, so jiggly, so unlike anyone else's. An appearance-obsessed teenager, I'd worry if I, too were doomed to inherit "the Horrie chin." (The answer is: yes. Yes, I was. Yes, I did.) Later, having done some Wild history research, I worried I might inherit Amy Faulkner Wild's dark under-eye circles, too. (Every morning, I try to remove what I choose to believe is eye makeup under my eyes. Every morning, dark circles still visible, I laugh at the vain and silly old woman in the bathroom mirror.)

I believe something deeper than vanity had been evident to thoughtful, five-year-old me that particular visit—although I will never know what it might have been. "Deeper than our faculties, more fundamental than our ideas or our images or our volitions, is the subsoil root of our being, this essence of the soul, this core of personality, which is indissolubly connected with a higher world of reality and is the ground of mystical experience," Rufus Jones declares.[14] Seventy years later, I can only speculate, with both an adult's logic and the sensibility of an emergent mystic, what might have caused me to think about death.

A Jungian might suggest that it had been the lamb. Lamb. Such a pungent, classic metaphor about death! (Which makes me wonder what Rufus Jones knew of Jungian archetypes.) And I know for a fact, because when my daughter Melissa, at age five, confronted me about lamb-the-meat being the same thing as lamb-as-Mary's-beloved-pet, that children are perfectly capable of understanding where their lamb stew or hamburger comes from—and that slaughter is involved. This horrifying understanding underlines why my daughter, Hope, and now, a grandson, Sam, and granddaughters, Ruby and Lilian, were or are (or are sometimes) vegetarians.

But I wonder if my five-year-old self hadn't realized that there had been something fundamentally tragic and ill-fated about my grandfather, Paul Revere Wild. Who wore bespoke suits, spoke with patrician accent, elegantly crooked his baby finger when he slurped his lamb stew. But who'd undeniably slurped. And smelled bad.

Sometimes my grandfather—my disabled grandfather—horrified me. His entire right side paralyzed from birth because, as family lore has it, the attending doctor had been drunk, his too-large head forever bore forceps marks proclaiming his violent entrance into this world.

As a child, I would not have understood what violence, what terrifying wrenching those deep crevices on either temple signified. (Years later, in my novel *Welling Up*, the fictional Rocco Pellegrino, a former member of Somerville's notorious Winter Hill Gang, bore those same marks. As my father observed, "You transplanted my father's head onto your character's!") Nor would I have understood how Grandpa's profound disabilities, both physical and, as my dad and I later speculated, cognitive, impacted his entire life. I wouldn't have known that my handsome, mustachioed great grandfather, Benjamin Franklin Wild, "Frank," had despised his first child, his profoundly disabled son. Or how, when my grandfather again mismanaged his Somerville-based coal and wood business, he'd go, hat in hand, to his parents' mansion on Highland Avenue where his tender-hearted mother, Amy, whose deep-pocketed Faulkner family dowry gave Frank Wild a generous start in the coal business, would write a generous check made out to her oldest son. Again.

Seated below that too-bright chandelier, what would I have noticed—and understood? I knew there was something off, I think. That despite the accoutrements of a well-off family—the polished silver tea set displayed on the dining room sideboard, the whirring, chiming grandfather clock in the front hall, my grandmother's baby grand piano (a wedding gift from her parents), the portraits of Luther and Martha Faulkner (Amy Faulkner Wild's mill-owning parents) hung over the horsehair couch in the living room—that despite all these lovely, smug things, my grandfather stumbled and lurched when he walked. He slurped his lamb stew—but no one said a word.

Did I sense that my grandmother's prodigious efforts to host happy, cheerful, family gatherings while caregiving her husband might have been exhausting? After she'd smoked her singular after-dinner cigarette that night, holding it between her thumb and index finger as she puffed, had Grandma realized she was too tired to read a story to Paul and me? Or to thump out a few rollicking favorites on the baby grand as the rest of us sang along? Instead of our usual Sunday night, after-dinner routine, had my beloved grandma, whose sobriquet I've chosen for myself, remained seated in the wing chair by the fireplace, quiet, pensive, weary? Melancholy? Did Grandma's possible *heaviness*, let's call it, heartily denied and unnamed, engender that moment on Route 2? Perhaps.

Much, much later, when my sister and I discussed our family, both of us beneficiaries of much wise counseling, both professional and from friends, Deborah remarked on another legacy of our grandfather's disability I might not have been able to recognize that Sunday. My sister believes that our father's shame at his father's condition had been all-too present in that fusty, wallpapered dining room. I think she's right.

My sister and I had very different relationships with our father. She could see and name and had experienced parts of him I saw but denied. So when she'd named Dad's shame, I'd nodded my head in instant recognition—yes. There it is. And it had always been there.

I can only imagine all the complicated, layered feelings my father harbored about his hat-in-hand father, whose disability meant, for example, that Frank Wild's chauffeur taught my father how to ride a bicycle. (His grandparents probably bought Dad that bike, too.) I imagine that, sometimes, like five-year-old me, my father had been horrified by his father—and then felt ashamed to feel that way.

Had I sensed my father's distress? His shame? I don't know. I know shame's potency, though, how, if ashamed, I flail about in a desperate attempt to feel something other than the feelings I feel. I know that, often, when I recall shameful moments, I involuntarily cry out—my horror of the harm I'd caused so distressing that I, in the moment, recoil. I know this, too: early days into this apprenticeship, my sister has red-flagged another masked feeling. Keep a lookout for shame, she's suggesting. It may be, like slithery lamb fat, attached to something else. "No one arrives on this earth encrusted with shame," Weller points out. "Rather, shame settles in our bones over time, accumulating during times of neglect and violation."[15]

What prompted that Route 2 realization? I don't know. What I believe, heart and soul, is that, like all of us, I, too, had been born with that "subsoil root of being, this essence of the soul, this core of personality," Rufus Jones described; "that of God," as George Fox put it.[16] And that tearful night, I'd felt something.

My beloved grandmother died in 1955, she in Medford, our family now in Fayetteville. There'd been no tears, no wailing, no ceremony, no obvious acknowledgment or shift in our family routine when she died. No wake, no gathering of family and friends to recall my grandmother and to tell stories, to laugh and cry together. No ceremonial sharing of food or drink. Nothing *buttery,* Grandma's highest praise for some culinary treat, had been served in her honor. None of us participated in any of the communal, shared, ritualized ways our species has always celebrated someone's life—and mourned. No, like any other routine business trip, my father packed a bag and joined his sister and Grandpa in Medford to make the final arrangements for Grandma's ashes to be buried at Mount Auburn Cemetery in Cambridge. Offstage. Away. Removed. (To be fair, since Ben would have been eight months old and Deborah would have been three, my parents may have reluctantly decided our family should stay home.)

Weaving my creation of loss and sorrow, my grandmother's soft, silver strands, the same shade of white as my own, are easily visible—identifiable. Significant. I'd adored my elegant, gifted, storyteller grandma, Florence Moulton Mirick Wild—her lamb stew not withstanding!

※※

"We are born expecting a rich and sensuous relationship with the earth and communal rituals of celebration, grief, and healing that keep us in connection with the sacred," Weller notes.[17] Soon after I began attending Friends Meeting at Cambridge, sensing this expectation, this need to celebrate and mourn communally, I showed up at a Quaker memorial for an older woman I barely knew. Arriving at the meeting's kitchen ahead of time to help prepare for the reception, I discovered that even ritual-wary Quakers sometimes perform almost pagan acts.

"[The deceased] loved licorice," one of her friends explained, pouring a bag of the black, stringy candy into a pretty bowl. "So I brought some for the reception."

What? Convinced that Quakers, especially the older women, were wise and deep and connected with the Divine in ways I would never be, I was startled by this unlikely contribution—but delighted. It seemed so wonderfully illogical! The deceased wouldn't be able to enjoy this special treat, right? So this offering made no sense. And yet, as I pondered during the silence of the memorial, by eating a piece of licorice—which I don't like—I'd be literally taking in something about the deceased. I'd somatically experience her; I'd taste a flavor she'd cherished. I'd cherish her.

**

Like Grandma, I am a storyteller, sometimes when telling stories to my grandchildren, sometimes when standing behind a mic at a storytelling slam, and sometimes during meeting for worship, a story will come to me that I am moved to share. So when I recall the "Thanatopsis" poem, I am remembering not only its basic, essential narrative, I am also remembering what presently, Zoom-dependent, I so miss: to be in a silent, large room with maybe a hundred people and to offer my words into that silence—to feel in that hush the meetinghouse's air as real a medium for me as clay or paint or human hair, to sense how my words are being taken in, and to learn a deeper truth by listening to that hush.

Here is the essential story: one day in my high school English class—in Lynchburg, Virginia—we'd read William Cullen Bryant's most famous poem, "Thanatopsis," which I'd instantly loved. That night, as we always did, my family ate dinner at precisely six o'clock, each of us, starting with five-year-old Benjy, sharing about our day. When it was my turn, I'd talked about this long poem we'd read in English class and gave its name. Immediately my father intoned, in the deep, sonorous voice he always used when quoting poetry, "So live, that when thy—"

"Yes! That's it!" I interrupted, delighted.

My father died in 2010; a few months later, during meeting for worship, sensing someone seated in that meetinghouse yearned to hear what I might share, I'd told that story. Its coda went something like this:

> This morning, thinking about that moment at my family's dinner table, I am filled with gratitude to realize what a gift my father gave me! For not only did he let me know that he and I shared a love for the same piece of writing; by quoting that poem, he'd let me know those words meant something to him, something sustaining, something he lived by. He let me know that he knew he was going to die. "So live" had informed how he chose to live. He'd lived. Knowing that fills me with joy.

**

My parents, my efficient parents, were planners. They wrote lists. They anticipated. A cautionary tale my father loved to tell featured a postal strike in Great Britain and how, because those Brits were not receiving their mail for several months, they'd spent money they'd ordinarily have spent on their electricity or phone bills on luxury items they couldn't afford.

"Didn't they realize the strike would eventually end?" my father would ask, shaking his head. "Didn't they realize that they'd have to pay those bills some day?" And then he'd pause, sigh: "No sense of future," he'd conclude—pronouncing that third word "fewcha," like anyone born in Somerville Hospital and raised in Somerville and Medford would. My parents had an inordinate sense of future. Which often meant giving little attention to the present. To the now.

Not surprisingly, then, my parents, who'd called death "The Inevitable," made careful end-of-life arrangements. They'd introduced Paul and me to the lawyer who would handle their estate; they'd driven us to the Cape Cod bank where their safe deposit box was located and given us keys. Having heard and read too many stories of bitter fights between siblings when divvying up their parents' estate, Mom and Dad were forever sharing stories of how other families decided who'd get what. (Not surprisingly, at least to me, the four of us, with welcomed input from our partners, had done just fine, thank you.) Briskly no-nonsense, our parents had done the necessary paperwork so as to donate their bodies to the University of Massachusetts Medical School. Well-trained "not to wallow," I hadn't allowed myself to consider what these grisly arrangements entailed. (Why lie: I still veer.) Ironically, because of some glitch at UMass, my father, whose high school grades hadn't been good enough to get into an Ivy League school, became a Harvard Medical School student's cadaver in 2010; in 2018, so did my mother's body.

What my mother and father couldn't do, of course, was to plan how to gracefully age, weaken, fail. But we four were lucky. They did age, weaken, fail gracefully. Slowly, incrementally, as if to provide their learning-impaired-when-it-came-to-grief children a long and gently sloped learning curve to accept "The Inevitable." "They let us down easy," one of us commented later. Over a couple decades, between nasty falls and hospitalizations and stints at rehab centers and yet another health scare and another "Is this the one?" and gradual cognitive decline, there were birthday parties and concerts and graduations and weddings and the arrival of great-grandchildren to distract all of us from what was coming. My parents continued to travel—even when they probably should have stayed home. They took classes; they both taught classes at Cape Cod Community College's Academy for Lifelong Learning. They lived.

A lovely memory from this hallowed time of gradual, parental decline: my daughter, Christina, who'd wanted to become a farmer and is now a gifted teacher, was about to graduate from Sterling College, a very small, environmentally conscious college in the exquisite village of Craftsbury Common, Vermont. Mom and Dad, who'd booked a room in the village inn so they could attend her graduation, had just driven up and parked the car.

My mother opened the passenger seat door, stepped down and arranged her silk scarf around her Horrie neck. She studied her perfect New England village and Northeast Kingdom surroundings, breathed in the incomparable Vermont air, and declared, "I knew this weekend would be wonderful. But I didn't know it would be so good for my soul!"

※※

Both Mom and Dad died alone. Like so many grieving families who have lost loved ones to COVID-19, we were denied the deathbed scene we'd always imagined: all of us gathered around; low, flickering light; gentle music or the lulling sound of flowing water piped in; final, whispered words of gratitude and love; the chance to stroke our father or mother's forehead, squeeze their hand, kiss them goodbye.

Instead, this: because a hospice bed was not yet available and my mother had been completely worn out, my father and I spent his last full night alive together at Cape Cod Hospital—a "fraught" night, he would have said. Confused, angry, agitated, he spent most of that night resisting the nurses and me; he repeatedly tried to get out of bed, even though he was dangerously weak and unstable. Scolded by the nurses and ever the sailor, even when dying, Dad extrapolated that he was on a cruise ship "run by harpies." I was not spared his wrath: "How long have you been in the Navy?" he asked disgustedly when I, too, tried to convince him to stay put. In the wee hours of the night, he fired me. "Your services are no longer required," he declared in his most formal, lofty, patrician voice. "You may present me with your bill in the morning."

Interspersed throughout that fraught night, though, were brief, moving interludes such as I'd always imagined. We sang together just like we'd done since I was a baby. As, indeed, the evening deepened, we sang "Abide With Me." Over and over. Sometimes, my father lay perfectly still, mesmerized, transfixed, watching something float in the air above his hospital bed. From his delighted smile, I know that whatever he watched must have been beautiful. And in a moment of lucidity just before dawn, he'd apologized: "I'm so sorry I'm putting you through this."

"Oh, Dad!" was all I could say, tearing up. How could I make clear to him that spending a tossed and roiled night on that cruise ship was a gift? And exactly where I wanted to be?

The next day, Dad was transferred to a nearby hospice; that evening, soon after my exhausted mother went home to sleep, he died. Alone. His body was sent off to Harvard Medical School, and my mother hosted the Pat Wild version of mourning—an open house with catered goodies.

Mysteriously, my deepest self understood that I didn't actually know how to grieve my father's death. Yes, I knew that eating an admittedly amazing brownie at my mother's open house did not speak to my condition; its chocolate-flavored deliciousness did not assuage my piercing pain. So what ought I to be doing? Something about crying, perhaps?

My father had loved opera, and so, in the spirit of eating that ceremonial piece of licorice, I absorbed his favorites. Like *Tosca* or Maria Callas's rendering of "Casta Diva." And I'd cry. (In that mourning period, I'd began a juicy biography of Callas, too, while scarfing down restorative chocolate as I read.) Sometimes, after weeping for a while, some over-the-top moment, some all out of proportion orchestration or high note held much too long would make me giggle. Because, well, opera! Who knew that sobbing interrupted by snickering—"Oh, Dad!" I'd complain, as if my father were personally responsible for Wagner's excesses or Pavarotti's showboating—would be so good for my soul?

An odd circumstance began soon after Dad died, a circumstance both logically explainable yet eerily spectral: I began to find pennies where I'd just vacuumed or where I'd been pretty sure there hadn't been a penny lying there four seconds ago. And, yes, pennies are everywhere. The eerie had more to do with how often these discoveries happened when I'd been particularly frightened, overwhelmed, anxious. Or sad.

The day we'd moved Mom's things out of her assisted-living apartment, for example, our work crew made several trips, back and forth and back and forth to load up a U-Haul; we schlepped a few key items to her tiny new room in the complex's nursing center, too. U-Haul loaded, Mom's new room cozy-fied, I'd made one more trip through the echoing rooms of Mom's now-empty apartment. I recalled her many moves as I inspected; how poignant this one was! About to close the door to her apartment, I looked down to see a shiny, new penny perfectly positioned on her apartment entrance's white carpet, the ubiquitous coin's coppery edge brushing up against the hallway's cinnamon-brown carpet. Poised there. At the very edge of Mom's last home.

"Thanks, Dad," I said aloud. I always thank my father out loud whenever I discover another penny in an illogical setting. Because I am always grateful for his presence in fraught times. I have always felt held and loved by my father.

And that continues.

**

And, instead, this: after several falls and now on a first-name basis with the town of Dennis's EMTs, my mother moved into an assisted-living complex on the Cape. A seamless move it seemed; several of her friends lived there, and she'd already been attending water aerobics classes at the complex's indoor pool. She'd loved buying furniture for her new home; she'd enjoyed dressing up for dinner. She'd relished her freedom, her autonomy, too—that she could walk through the complex hallways to the pool and no longer had to deal with annoyances like a smoke detector needing a new battery. When my husband offered to help her with her paperwork, she told him, "I actually enjoy writing checks." And we'd believed her.

But one Saturday morning at nine o'clock, the same day and time I always called her, I got a recorded message saying her phone wasn't working. A little sleuthing and I learned why: Mom hadn't paid her phone bill. And then there was the story she told us, laughing, about how she'd been fired from her volunteer job at the complex's little convenience store—she'd loved chitchatting with her customers—because she couldn't make change.

Oh.

So here it was, our brilliant mother was slipping—not unexpected, but nevertheless heartbreaking. Had we missed other signs of slippage; had we trusted her too much? We didn't know—but quickly arranged with the complex's nursing staff for someone to come to her apartment every day to help with her medications. After being hospitalized at Cape Cod Hospital for a mysterious ailment, this latest hospitalization had been followed by a long and listless stay in the assisted-living complex's rehabilitation wing. Evaluated by its staff, our mom was deemed unable to safely live in her apartment and immediately transferred to the complex's nursing center. Gently guided by the center's social worker—who sometimes served as our family therapist—we four read up on dementia.

Soon after Mom had been transferred to the nursing center, my husband and I drove to the Cape to visit. After lunch, Mom, who now needed a wheelchair, felt tired, so we wheeled her back to her shared room for a nap. Loathe to transfer her from her wheelchair to her bed, however, I'd walked down the hall to the nurses station; six or eight other residents in wheelchairs waited there, too. But when I politely asked for some help "when it's convenient," I'd emphasized; instead, the nurse ignored the waiting crowd in front of him and immediately walked back with me to hoist Mom onto her bed.

So that's how it works?

In our readings and conversations with the center's social worker, one thing seemed clear: to move an aging parent with dementia into an adult child's home was a recipe for burnout and disaster—particularly if the relationship between the parent and grown-child caregiver had been fraught. I'd appreciated the wisdom of this; my brothers and sister did, too.

A hastily arranged family conference, and we all agreed: Mom now needed long-term care and would receive better care if family members consistently but randomly showed up. Paul, who lived on the Cape and had patiently bolstered both Mom and Dad through twenty long years of health scares and crises, was still working. My sister and I, both living in greater Boston, had more flexible schedules. So we moved Mom to a long-term care facility, aka a nursing home, in nearby Cambridge where, bonus, Mom had a private room. We hung her favorite paintings and family pictures on the walls, we lined the ample windowsill with plants, we filled a bookcase with her favorite books and photo albums, we bought a cheerful quilt for her bed.

Some expert tweaking of her anxiety/depression meds, daily cheered on as she did physical therapy, delighted to go for wheelchair "walks" along Neville Center's paved, wooded paths to a little pond where she could watch turtles and a great blue heron, or wheeled along Fresh Pond, Cambridge's fenced-off reservoir, to say hello to dog-walking Cantabrigians, Mom perked up.

"I can't say I'm happy," she told us. "But I'm content. That's the right word."

Again, we four were lucky, incredibly lucky. A lifetime of losses and regrets and slights and hurts and painful memories were miraculously scrubbed clean by dementia; Mom was content. Sweetly content. Sometimes, when I arrived to her room, there she'd be, completely still, sitting in her wheelchair, an opened paperback on her lap, deep in thought, smiling.

"I've just been thinking about what a wonderful life I have had," she'd say.

My sister confided, "Sometimes I want to say to her, 'I don't know what you've done with my real mother, but whoever you are, you're a very sweet old lady. So I plan to keep on visiting you!'"

This is hard to write: Mom's day-to-day life at Neville Center, living with querulous, agitated, or comatose old people, some of whom wore adult diapers and smelled despite the diligent staff's efforts, must have been frightening—even before this pandemic. Yet she never complained. She never asked, "Why am I here?" or "Why can't I live with you?"

Stiff-upper-lipped, Classy Lady Mom endured; she took refuge in her cozy room; she frequently napped. Less impaired than most of the other residents, Mom consistently won at bingo, a classically senior-citizen activity that Old Mom would have sneered at but Content Mom thoroughly enjoyed. Every week she won, she would add another costume jewelry necklace or pendant or gaudy bracelet to the bingo-winning prizes she already wore; Content Mom became a laden Christmas tree. (I'd rather not think about who'd previously owned those flashy, shiny things or how this seemingly endless supply ended up at Neville Center.)

She noticed when an aide was pregnant and asked me to buy a baby gift. She made friends with another resident, Beatrice, a quiet woman with a lovely, gentle smile. She and Mom often sat together for meals and at bingo; Beatrice won pretty regularly, too. When Beatrice died, Mom took a while to absorb this loss but, eventually, asked me to do something.

"Her church was very good to her, very important," Mom noted—a little wistfully, I thought. "Maybe I should make a contribution." And vis-a-vis my husband, who'd begun paying Mom's bills, she did.

One bright summer day, a couple of years before she died, I'd been pushing her wheelchair up the little hill near the soccer field when, out of the blue, Mom mentioned *The Divine Secrets of the Ya Ya Sisterhood* and how much she'd loved that book. Pretty inured to her random thoughts and obscure references, I didn't ask her what prompted her to bring up that book; as a writer and as the daughter who'd been on that cruise ship with my dying father, my mother's randomness, her metaphor-rich references intrigued me.

"I can get you a copy of that book if you'd like to read it again, Mom," I'd said.

She twisted around in her wheelchair seat to look at me, sweaty-palmed and breathing hard: "You're so good to me, Patricia. Was I this good to you growing up?"

I debated how to answer. Should I tell her, "Well, Mom, actually, sometimes—" before experiencing another in-breaking: "Why would you say something like that to her?" my better angels coached. "What would be accomplished?"

And I remembered that wonderful quote from Lily Tomlin: "Forgiveness means giving up all hope for a better past."

What a gift I have just been given, I realized. The past is done. Gone. She's erased it. I can erase it, too. Why not? Right now. My life can begin today. Right this minute.

"Of course you were," I assured her, pushing her past the lush-green soccer field, newly mowed.

As I much later realized, *The Divine Secrets of the Ya Ya Sisterhood*, the book she'd randomly referenced, is about the difficult relationship and eventual reconciliation between a beautiful, unfulfilled mother who drinks too much and her oldest child—a daughter! The ineluctable bond between a mother and her daughter was in the air that forgiving, inbreaking moment, I think, as real as the smell of freshly cut grass.

Prompted by love, my mother and I began to improvise a new story together, just like my father once made up delightful stories about Timothy the Squirrel when my siblings and I were young. Here we were, she and I, living into this new story. Living. It would be a bittersweet story entwined with both love and grief; we knew that. We both knew how this story would end.

But who, exactly, was this story's main character? Who was Content Mom? This sweet old lady Deb enjoyed visiting? I only know how to put Mom's emergent personhood into the language—and the construct—of my faith.

Mom, the essential Patricia Lillian Horrie Wild, had been born with innate sweetness, an undeniable Inner Light, that of God, a soul. Dementia unburdened her of the pain, loss, sorrows, regrets, and shame she'd lugged around for most of her life; dementia tore up my anxious and overwhelmed mother's to-do lists and tossed them in the recycle bin. What remained was what had always been within her, what had always been her deepest self, that shimmering interiority she'd brought to Christina's college graduation.

Early Quakers often talked of "the refiner's fire." Another useful metaphor to explain Mom's seeming transformation might be that dementia burned off the dross and allowed my mother's pure, unalloyed self to come forth. To shine forth like gold.

A story to illustrate this construct: many, many Augusts ago, I'd attended New England Yearly Meeting at Maine's Bowdoin College, a gathering of Quakers living in New England that, as you might deduce, meets once a year, in early August. That year, I'd opted to attend a three-day workshop called "Meeting Jesus Again for the First Time." [18] Over the years, I'd discovered that attending the yearly meeting's three-day workshops offered a wonderful opportunity to more deeply delve into a chosen topic—and I certainly wanted to learn more about the Quaker take on "Jesus the Carpenter's Son." Spending three days together also offered a wonderful opportunity to meet and to better know other New England Quakers.

On the third and final day, just as the workshop was winding down, a woman knocked on our classroom's door: "May I come in?" she asked.

What transpired was extraordinary: that woman entered, introduced herself, wanted us to know that her mother had recently died, and she was now moved to tell others what she'd experienced. Our class, having just shared many thoughtful, probing hours together, got very quiet, the kind of quiet that can happen when a group of people has created a web of trust and honesty and caring among themselves. We silently held the space; we breathed in harmony; we took in her words.

Which went something like this: "And then my mother said, 'Oh! Look! We're ruffled! We're all inside out! Our inside is filled with light!'"

That dying mother's glimpse of Light-filled inner selves—how the word "veil" is sometimes used to describe the silk-thin delineation between living and dying—to me, that deathbed vision and eponymous metaphor suggests a thinning process, to use Mom's word in a completely different context. Our inner light may become more visible.

And in Mom's last year, that thinning process became more and more apparent. She'd report that my father began to visit her more and more. Waking from a nap, she'd be confused; more fully awake, she'd confess she was having a hard time differentiating between her dreams and reality. And, like Dad, she began to sprinkle boat and trip and journey metaphors into her speech.

And then, in August of 2018, Mom's and our luck ran out; her last three months were pain-filled, her ninety-five-year-old body wracked with muscle cramps. Meds and heating pads and other soothing comfort-care measures would alleviate these intense and random spasms; nothing stopped them. She lay in bed tense with fearful anticipation for the next seizing.

Sometimes, mercifully, when whatever med she'd been given let her sleep, I'd sit by her bed for an hour or so. Sometimes my "that of God" connected with her "that of God," and those soulful moments were precious. Sometimes, I'd experience that profound deep-knowing that there was nowhere else I was supposed to be, there was absolutely nothing else I was supposed to do but to be right where I was, seated beside her, singing to her. I prayed her pain would be alleviated; I prayed Neville's staff would concoct some miraculous, medical cocktail to stop her pain. Given how well they'd medicated her depression and anxiety, I'd half-believed some medical intervention was possible.

But there was to be no miraculous cocktail. With no name to label Mom's unbearable condition, no established treatment or protocol, I worried we'd missed something.

"Mom took her bed," my sister suggested later. Mom was ready to die, Deb meant. I wasn't so sure and, oldest child, felt irrationally uber-responsible. As always.

Did we miss something? (Who, exactly, is this we?)

"Why can't you do something?" Mom begged. The best something, we all agreed, would be hospice's palliative care—but on October 11, the night before hospice was to begin, Mom died in her sleep. Alone.

"I am numb," I wrote in my journal the next morning. "I am sad she died alone—yet have the sense that's how she wanted it. To spare us. To not even deal with hospice. Although [someone from hospice] met with Mom yesterday. What did that mean for her? I'll never know."

Written only hours after she'd died, this acknowledgment, this irrefutable not ever knowing what that visit from a hospice staff person had meant felt real and deep—and right. Sitting with this acknowledgment, taking that nonnegotiable realization in, I found the deep sadness I was supposed to feel. As time went on, though, as life around me moved into shortening days, into bare trees and icy winds, into Thanksgiving, into Christmas, into New Year's, I began to worry that I was mourning my mother all wrong. Why wasn't I feeling that same piercing pain I'd felt when my father died? Why wasn't I missing her?

Had my enormous relief that she was no longer in pain overtaken or masked my grief? After a lifetime of denial, was I too numbed to experience sadness? Or, worse, was I still holding on to old pain and hurt and therefore not able to access feelings of sadness, loss, that for the first time in my entire life, I had no mother?

I judged myself. And gave myself an "F."

Although my journal entries during that period hint that I'd dimly sensed what my soul already knew, it wasn't until a few months later, when I read *The Five Invitations: Discovering What Death Can Teach Us About Living Fully* by Frank Ostasecki, that I truly understood.

It was the passage about Jeff and Samantha, a husband and wife both in their forties, that put words and meaning to my puzzling, substandard response to my mother's death. Beautifully, insightfully, Ostasecki describes how, over the course of several days, this loving couple interacts as Jeff begins to fail—to *dissolve*—Ostasecki's wonderful verb encapsulating death's thinning process.

Jeff exhales but does not inhale again. "A stillness and ease embraced us. I felt it as warmth and sensed a luminosity, a sort of brilliance. After some time, Samantha spoke out loud, as if talking to the space more than to me. 'I thought I was losing him, but he is everywhere.'"[19]

My mother is everywhere: when I look in a mirror or at my Zoom square, there she is. When I grab a yellow legal pad to take notes, there she is. When I drink a glass of wine and then crave chocolate, when I become so absorbed in a book that, if interrupted, I look up and around me as if to ask, "How did I get here?" there she is. When I make a to-do list and briskly check off each completed task, there she is. She is right beside me, wherever I am, whenever I note "the quality of the light." Because she always did. As she'd done a thousand other things, some of which I now do, too. How can I miss her? She's here. She's always been here.

∗∗

"Sometimes I'm not sure if, when we say 'Quaker values,' we don't actually mean WASP values," someone from my meeting lamented once. I get that. As John Calvi[20] recently quipped, "If George Fox had been Sicilian—?" And he'd shaken his head, marveling at how different Quakerism would have turned out. But Fox, one of the founders of the Religious Society of Friends, had been born in Drayton-in-the-Clay, in Leicester, England, in 1624.

"Be still and cool in your own mind and spirit from your own thoughts, and then you will feel the principle of God to turn your mind to the Lord God, from whom life comes," Fox advises.[21] Hearkening to Fox's advice, when someone we love dies, Quakers do not rend our clothing or scream and cry. Not publicly, anyway. If we rend or scream and cry, we do so in our own homes. A pre-pandemic version of social distancing, my meeting community mails notes and cards. We'll call to let the bereaved know that their grief and loss are acknowledged and held in the Light. After my mother died, my friend Dinah Starr mailed me a sheaf of wonderful poems she'd found comforting after her mother died, for example. This paper version of the dropped-off casserole or the Victorian funereal baked meats I found delicious—food for my soul.

In that same spirit of still and cool, a Quaker memorial meeting is usually scheduled several months after someone has died to give the bereaved family ample time to reflect, cry, cope, plan. So, although Mom died in October, her memorial meeting was scheduled for the following April, close to her birthday.

Not surprisingly, Mom had spent a good deal of time thinking about her funeral and where it should be held. "There should be a fireplace," she'd sometimes insist. "And comfortable chairs." In search of just the right space, we'd toured the Cape Cod Community College building where many of her and Dad's Academy for Lifelong Learning classes were held; nothing suited. She'd also loved the idea of holding the celebration for her life at a parking lot overlooking Cape Cod's Sessuit Harbor's channel, a stretch of water that connects a large marina to Nantucket Sound. Mom's plan was to set up a tent in the vicinity of a tall pole at one end of the parking lot; this pole supported an osprey's nest she and Dad had loved to watch.

And I'd understood: one of the happy memories Mom would recall from her Neville wheelchair were the years she and Dad lived on a thirty-six-foot, double-cabin, trawler yacht, the *Katie Brown*, and cruised up and down the Inland Waterway. This parking lot site she'd wanted for her funeral, right on a channel, powerboats gliding by, their low-pitched, gurgling inboard-motor sound a beloved memory; yes, I could understand why she chose this osprey-graced location.

As the clerk of my meeting's Memorials Committee for many years, however, and someone who'd interacted with many, many families, I'd nixed her idea. Gently: "I see why you want this. I know how much you and Dad loved that spot. But, Mom! Many of your friends are old. They are not going to want to use a porta potty—which we would definitely have to provide—and they won't be comfortable sitting on rented chairs on a parking lot's uneven ground. They're going to want ramps. Easily accessible restrooms. Cushioned chairs."

I hadn't said aloud the obvious: "And besides, you won't be there, Mom. Your children will actually decide how this will happen."

And, over time, we did. My sister belongs to a gorgeous, white-frame and steepled Unitarian Universalist church in nearby Waltham, a quintessentially New England church not unlike First Parrish in Stow, located on Stow's town green, the Unitarian church we'd attended when Deb was a baby. I'd met Deb's minister and knew he would do a lovely job. Holding a memorial service for Mom at Waltham's First Parish and following the same liturgy the four of us had grown up with seemed appropriate. On reflection, however, Deb realized she had little energy to organize such an event.

Surprisingly, I did. Looking back, I think my unexpected energy came from an undeniable, adolescent part of me that, once upon a time, considered becoming a Unitarian minister. At fifteen, sixteen, I'd seen myself choosing hymns and appropriate readings, officiating at weddings and funerals, laboring over sermons, offering pastoral care. I'd be good at it. Designing Mom's memorial, choosing, for example, to close this memorial by singing, "I Love You Truly," my parents' song and the song I'd quietly sung to my sleeping mom in her last few months, would serve as my one-off ministerial career.

Some of that untapped energy, I think, was about my wanting to ameliorate a collective sense of unfinished business: that many of us who'd mourned my father, all of us hard-wired for ritual,[22] had found Mom's open house for Dad unsatisfying. Many in my family understood that we'd needed to all be in the same room at the same time; we needed to sing together, a Wild tradition; we needed to laugh and cry together—to perform whatever rituals were appropriate—such as the ceremoniously shaking of hands with those around us when a Quaker memorial ends. (As I write this, I think of the many, many mourning families throughout the world who have been denied their own and much-needed rituals during this pandemic. And hold them in the Light.)

Most of all, whether the descendants of Florence or Al Wild, our family needed to tell stories. And we did. Unscripted, unplanned, when moved to speak, people stood to share some anecdote about Mom. Grandma. Aunt Pat. Mrs. Wild. *Nana* to her great-grandchildren. I told the story of how I'd criticized her once for spending so much time planning, living in the "fewcha": "I do take time to smell the roses, Patricia!" she'd snapped. "I just smell them faster than most people."

As had been suggested at the beginning of the memorial by my dear friend, Wendy Sanford, who had care of meeting, those who spoke allowed some quiet between each message for some breathing space so that whatever had been offered could be heard, taken in, to resonate, be. As so often happens at a Quaker memorial, that we were all there to celebrate the same person unified us in a way that doesn't seem to happen as frequently during a regular meeting for worship. We all spoke out of the same, shared Spirit; we all drew from the same Source.

How ironic that Mom's funeral service centered on storytelling! "Not her long suit," her bridge-wiz mother, Lil, might have put it. In truth, like her appreciation for her friend Beatrice's churchgoing, although she'd respected others' connection to a spiritual community, Mom would not have felt comfortable with whatever service or ritual her children chose to celebrate her life. She endlessly talked about where her funeral service should be; I don't think she cared much about what would happen once her mourners arrived—nor had stipulated how this celebration of her life should go. And as someone who'd prided herself on smelling the roses faster than everyone else, any service lasting an entire hour would have probably seemed much too long to her.

In the months leading up to her memorial, I'd consider what sort of ceremony, ritual, funeral service, memorial, or celebration of her life Pat Wild would have actually wanted. And it came to me. She would have wanted all her mourners to ceremoniously eat chocolate ice cream with a long-handled spoon—also known as an iced teaspoon. Ten, fifteen minutes, tops! That's all this delicious, Pat Wild-friendly ritual would require.

In honor of this imagined but appropriate ceremony, on the day of Mom's memorial, I went into the FMC kitchen and took down six cobalt-blue goblets from the cabinet's top shelf. (The FMC kitchen cabinet is stacked, floor to ceiling, with lovely serving dishes and glassware and pretty bowls like the one used for licorice at my first memorial. I'd had my eye on those blue goblets for months!) Each ice cream dish filled with sprigs of forsythia and one or two daffodils from our garden—apparently I was the kind of minister who did the flowers, too—I placed an adorned glass on every windowsill of Friends Meeting at Cambridge's meetinghouse; a private joke, an Easter Egg.[23] And deeply satisfying.

Until we can grieve for our planet we cannot love it—grieving is a sign of spiritual health. But it is not enough to weep for our lost landscapes; we have to put our hands in the earth to make ourselves whole again. Even a wounded world is feeding us. Even a wounded world holds us, giving us moments of wonder and joy. I choose joy over despair. Not because I have my head in the sand, but because joy is what the earth gives me daily and I must return the gift.
Braiding Sweetgrass: Indigenous Wisdom, Scientific Knowledge, and the Teaching of Plants, Robin Wall Kimmerer[76]

With Hope Yet with Tears

After driving through other parts of the country—rural Maine, for example, or that stretch of I-65 between Indianapolis and Louisville—my husband and I will note how it's just *easier* that we live in congested, woefully-lacking-in-parks-or-open-spaces Somerville. And we agree how heartbreaking it must be to live in one of the farmhouses or trailers or subdevelopments we've passed where, daily, it must seem, urban infringements encroach, closer and closer, propagating overnight. Like those ubiquitous self-storage units, ugly as prisons and so mystifying, popping up and spreading like kudzu in the middle of what had once been forests or fields of soybeans and corn.

(Why do so many people need so much extra storage space? Does this question reveal I don't understand something very basic and fundamental about my country?)

Save those childhood years when we'd lived in Fayetteville and our house abutted a large and accessible forest with a pond and amphibian-rich swampland and meandering horse trails maintained by the riding stable nearby, for most of my life, nature has been someplace you drive to—like Cape Cod's beaches or the national parks we'd visited on our Stow to LA trip or the series of sailboats we'd chartered to spend family vacations aboard.

For most of my life, nature has always been someplace you drive to—and then overcome. Although there were precious, quiet, soul-nourishing moments under sail, to employ wind power to travel from Point A to Point B meant the us on the sailboat versus the them of wind and current and tides. (How startling it had been to take all day to arrive at Point B only to drive back to Point A in less than an hour!) At Girl Scout camp in the Adirondacks, army-surplus-gear-equipped as if pubescent soldiers, we Girl Scouts slept in army tents, we ate from GI mess kits, we attacked, we tamed nature with our Girl Scout jackknives and nifty, olive-colored, collapsible shovels. Trenches to dig and brush to clear, we had no time for reverence, for gawking, for moments of wonder and joy. Spurred on by our counselors, many of them gym teachers during the school year, we girls got deliciously dirty. We grunted; we heaved fallen branches; we endured long, sweaty hikes, "No whining, scouts," took long slurps from Army-surplus canteens slung across our still-flat chests. We wiped our noses on our filthy sleeves like boys. We survived nature.

Unlike many climate activists, I do not mourn the lost landscapes of my childhood. I no longer live where I grew up; their particular and painful loss has not been my own. I do, however, mourn the loss of the star-rich, nighttime sky of my childhood. On clear nights, right in my own backyard, I'd marveled at the Milky Way; I stood silent and deeply moved. I connected with something vast, far away, impossible to accurately enumerate, something much greater than myself. Those sightings convinced eight-year-old me, fourteen-year-old me, nineteen-year-old me that God existed—as a noun, as the Creator, as the deity.

But in the face of bleaching coral reefs and the extinction of countless species both great and small, in the face of deadly heat waves and flash floods and more violent hurricanes, in the face of all the ways our wounded planet urges us to acknowledge, pay attention, act—even before I'd begun this apprenticeship, to grieve for those pre-light-pollution moments from my childhood seemed thin. Like a single strand of light-brown hair, perhaps, found inside the grubby, white sailor's cap, purchased from an Army-Navy store in Syracuse that I'd worn constantly at Girl Scout camp or while sailing, its ample brim turned down to resemble a cloche.

No, as an adult moved to work on climate action, it had not been visceral grief I'd drawn upon. My come-to-Jesus moment centered on my 3 a.m. terror of the devastated world my grandchildren would inherit.

"May you be ancestors worth descending from," Annie sometimes enjoins at the end of our yoga class. (She's quoting her mentor, Martín Prechtel, Indigenous writer, teacher, artist.) Prompted by my fierce love for my descendants, several years ago, I banded together with other climate activists, most of us white, well-educated, and well-off women, and joined Mothers Out Front.[24] We entreated our family and friends to join us; we got important legislation passed here in Massachusetts; we collectively switched our electricity provider to all-renewables like wind and hydropower. In 2014, we joined with over three hundred thousand other climate activists from all over the world at The People's Climate March in New York City. Filled with overflowing joy that two grandchildren could experience this incredible event, I danced with Brooklyn-based Dmitri and Ruby down the middle of Broadway!

Sometimes in history, that long arc of the moral universe bends a little closer toward justice when, like that glorious

People's Climate March of 2014, hundreds of thousands of people are called into action. And sometimes, what we're called to do to help heal the world has our own name on it.

When Fossil Free Somerville, an energetic group of young, savvy Somerville organizers, began their initiative to persuade the Somerville Retirement Board to divest from fossil fuel investment, FFS wanted to find a couple of pensioners willing to show up at the board's meetings and at City Hall to speak in favor of this initiative. A former teacher at the Somerville Public School's adult learning center, I, indeed, receive a monthly check from that board. A check with my name on it. So after some discernment—what if divestment is a terrible idea and there goes my monthly check?—I signed on. A retired firefighter signed on, too. We joined FFS. And showed up. We wore orange T-shirts demanding "Divest Now," and rain or shine, we held signs in front of City Hall. We attended meetings in the city council chamber. We prevailed. (Locally, anyway.[25])

But I now understand that my soul yearned for more—and more than once whispered, "When we say 'we,' who, exactly, are we?" I only half-heard. Four or five years later, when someone from my Quaker meeting asked this question out loud—we'd been laboring with our annual "State of Society" report—I heard this gentle probing with instant recognition. Yes! Who, exactly, is this *we*? Who's not here? Who's not showing up? Who's not able to show up? Whose wisdom and life experience and insights are not being listened to? As my dear friend, Dr. Owen Cardwell, observed, "We can't get along until we have an understanding that we're equals at the table."[26] Who's not sitting at that table? And why?

Like many of my generation, I'd become a social activist during the Vietnam War. Furious at that unjust and unnecessary war, I'd become a peace activist. And had been *siloed*, as we now say. (And smugly righteous.) Although Martin Luther King Jr. stressed how interrelated and interconnected racism, militarism, and economic injustice were,[27] again, I only half-heard. But like that State of Society *we* moment, the right words were made available, the right words which, to paraphrase Isaac Penington, "God sowed in my heart."[28]

My first glimpse of those right words happened in the early nineties when I'd attended a statewide meeting of teachers working in Massachusetts shelters and held at Worcester's Catholic Charities. (I later discovered that Grandma had grown up just a few blocks away!) Styrofoam coffee cup in hand, I was waiting for the meeting to begin when I caught sight of a sign made from cut-out fabric letters stitched onto a large piece of crimson-colored burlap that hung in the back of that agency's fusty meeting room. The hand-stitched letters spelled out, "If you want peace, work for justice." That this prophetic advice appeared in a room graced by the spirit of Dorothy Day and Sister Helen Prejean and Oscar Romero gave those sewn words added value. Ever since, enjoined to work for peace for all, justice for all, a livable planet for all, every Sunday morning I ask myself, "What am I called to do to help mend this world?" during meeting for worship.

Writing this in the midst of a pandemic making starkly clear the state of this country, I find myself asking a radically different question: What can my soul teach me? And when I ask this question, I begin to write from a different place.

My soul longs to connect with other souls— like joyously dancing down Broadway with my grandchildren and thousands of others. As I begin to understand this dynamic, I better understand why the small, fossil-fuels voluntary tax group I joined less than a year ago has become so important to my life!

Here's how it works: seven people, including my husband and me, all of us members of Friends Meeting at Cambridge, have agreed to meet quarterly. Ahead of time, we each compute what we owe based on whatever carbon-footprint calculation formula most suits our particular needs.[29] We take turns researching possible organizations or groups doing important work on a chosen topic—like water or trees—and the night we meet, over tea and goodies and after some silent worship, we collectively decide where to mail our checks. Members of a large and sometimes unwieldy Quaker meeting, we're finding this small group discernment process delightful! But there's more to these quarterly experiences than how smoothly we're able to reach unity. What I'm now realizing is that we're apparently fulfilling a deep, fundamental need we all share—a need I am just beginning to recognize: "Only connect." Which is why, I guess, when we get together, we take turns declaring, "You know something? Not sure why, but this group makes me so happy!"

At our most recent Zoom meeting, prompted by my emergent embrace of climate-change mitigation work as justice work, I'd suggested we send our pooled checks to Cosecha, "a nonviolent movement fighting for permanent protection, dignity, and respect for the eleven million undocumented immigrants in the United States,"[30] our checks specifically targeted to support undocumented immigrants facing financial hardship due to COVID-19.

When I'd presented this idea, there had been some pushback from our little group; some members rightfully pointed out that we'd previously supported organizations providing direct service to mitigate climate change—One Tree Planted or The New England Grassroots Environmental Fund, for example. I found myself strangely reluctant to spell out to the members of my fossil-fuels voluntary tax group the horrifying connectivity between climate change, racism, and economic injustice—and how this pernicious interrelatedness so radically impacted undocumented immigrants right now. I simply didn't want to have to explain.

Why? Because, I think, my soul longed for that little group, so precious, so important to me to just get it. Please, dear friends, please see this gestalt the same way I am seeing it. And, eventually, each of us in our own little Zoom box, our Inner Guides connected. We all agreed.

A disturbing and confusing fact: pre-pandemic, what had my husband and I most atoned for? What comprised the largest percentage of our quarterly carbon tax check? Airline trips to visit far-flung grandchildren and family members. The people we are now aching to hug.

So here is a paradox, confusing, messy, and profoundly disquieting. "In order to care for the soul, we may have no choice but to open our hearts wide enough to contain that tension and polytheistically give both needs a hearing," writes Thomas Moore.[31]

I'm listening.

Now, listening to a deeper part of myself longing to sit at Owen's table, I'm acutely missing Somerville's Sanctuary City Standing Committee's weekly meetings. Seated around a capacious City Hall table, the Trump administration's racist and cruel immigration policies our ongoing concern, whatever we discussed, be it public charge[32] or how these policies traumatize undocumented immigrant families, had been horrifying, painful, real. (Sadly, as I write this, the Biden administration doesn't seem much of an improvement!) Yet, just as I'd experienced while seated beside my sleeping mother in the weeks before she died, there was nowhere else I was supposed to be; there was absolutely nothing else I was supposed to do but to be right where I was. A volunteer community member, I had been so grateful to weekly hold the space, to prayerfully listen and to learn from the SC/SC committee members, many of them women of color, all of them thoughtful, wise, and focused on the needs of our city's residents. All our residents. We.

So when a fundraising opportunity to raise money for a legal defense fund for immigrants arose, and, as city employees, many of the group's members prohibited from participating in such a fundraising effort, that initiative had my name on it, too.

I'd loved our we. And I await, impatiently, for when we can again meet around that capacious table.

**

Broader still than we is all. All-encompassing, one. Wholeness. "All my relations," as the Lakota say. The Hindu *Om*. Or Aum, "representing the union of mind, body, and spirit."[33] Or, as Annie sometimes explains Om, "That which when something is removed, nothing is changed," a one-word cosmology that comforted me after my father died and would shape how I'd mourned my mother.

As I write these all-embracing, encompassing words, I picture my dear friend, Lynn Lazar, who died in 2019, her right hand reaching up and circling, encompassing: "We're not separate," she'd remind anyone who would listen, her hand continuing to circle as she spoke. "We're all connected. We think we are separate, but we're not!"

My soul knows this. Earth knows this. Thomas Merton knew this. All-that-is, this wondrous universe knows this. But I have spent most of my life not understanding what Lynn was telling us. I have only understood a binary world. When wandering along the horse trails in the Fayetteville woods, I had been accompanied; I understand that, now. There had been a wordless presence present in those Fayetteville woods. I had been surrounded by and was in community with and enveloped within All—All above me, around me, under my sneakers, inside me. In that dappled quiet, alone, breathing in rotting, rich, humus-y smells I could only name *woodsy*, I had been briefly gifted with a deeper knowledge.

I see, now, that I'd had intimations of something different. In my Unitarian Sunday school class at Syracuse's May Memorial Church, I'd dreamily stare at an opened textbook, *From Long Ago and Many Lands*.[34] On the inside cover and first page and printed in red ink had been a Chinese proverb written in sixteen different languages: "Under the sky all men are one family." As our class droned on around me, I'd get lost in those red lines and squiggles on a tan background, some written horizontally, some vertical. And briefly I'd sense Om's union, wholeness.

There is plenty of binary in this memory, though: Me/ all those people who speak and write in Tamil or Sanskrit, languages I'd never heard of. Or All of Us Under the Sky/ Everything beyond Earth's Atmosphere.

Latent, vague, never named, was the ever-present binary I grew up with, the us/them as in my white family and them, people of color who speak Baganda or Urdu and who, as we'd been taught in our all-white Sunday school class, were just like us but were, in fact, never really real. Through our station wagon's windows, our family saw people of color en route to James Street in downtown Syracuse or, a few years later, while driving through Black neighborhoods to Lynchburg's tiny, exquisite Unitarian church, perched on downtown's steep hill overlooking the James River. The millions of people represented by red squiggles in a Sunday school textbook or viewed from a car window were as mysterious and as alien to me as everything beyond Earth's atmosphere. As if to concretize my limited thinking, in graduate school, one of my instructors actually speculated that, since our brain functions much like a computer, humans are hard-wired to think binary. Us/them, good/bad, and white/black is our destiny, he suggested.

There have been other moments in my life when, as we'd said in the sixties, I'd grokked[35] Wholeness—full, deep, rich, grateful moments when, like Robin Kimmerer describes in *Sweetgrass*, I'd been brought to my knees with wonder and joy. I distinctly remember the first: on a foothill of the Sierra de Mijas mountains in southern Spain's Andalusia region, my first husband and I split a capsule of mescaline that we washed down with a Coke—and I experienced an afternoon of Oneness, of connection to All, deeply felt and never to be forgotten. But I'd also suffered brief but frightening moments of skewed perception. So, when the peyote-like chemicals slowly wore off and the purple-rich, color-separated shadows around us lengthened, I'd felt relieved—and disinclined to repeat that experience.

And then came a series of books: the first had been an antidote to what that grad school instructor suggested—an antithetical-to-binary-thinking book I'd read in the eighties, *The Origin of Consciousness in the Breakdown of the Bicameral Mind* by Julian Jaynes. Or, as Hope, Allison, and Christina called that black-and-white, dust-jacketed hardcover: "That book you're always reading, Mom, that tells everything about what it's about by its cover." Jaynes speculates that when our brain's two hemispheres communicate with one other, wondrous understanding is possible.

Heavy! Far out! Or as seventeenth-century George Fox would put it: "And I experienced great openings."

Two books I read in 2018: a novel, *The Overstory* by Richard Powers, a hefty, brilliant bestseller my friends and I shared, and the nonfiction *Braiding Sweetgrass: Indigenous Wisdom, Scientific Knowledge, and the Teachings of Plants* by Robin Wall Kimmerer, recommended by Annie, offered further insights. And I finally began to dimly understand what Lynn Lazar and Indigenous people and poets and mystics understand—and what I had been briefly shown on an Andalusian foothill.

So you can imagine my excitement in late March of 2019, when Harvard University announced that both Powers and Kimmerer had been invited to speak at a free and open-to-the-public conversation to be facilitated by Terry Tempest Williams, another well-known nature writer and the writer-in-residence at Harvard Divinity School that year. And why, notoriously early, I'd been even more prompt than usual, knowing how immensely popular those two books were—one of the first to wait outside the Yenching Auditoriuum, a lecture hall of the Harvard-Yenching Institute. Other *Overstory* and *Braiding Sweetgrass* fans were already there; some I'd known from my climate activist days; a few early birds attend my Quaker meeting. As the crowd waiting in the hallway and our collective excitement grew, the grad students serving as ushers eyed us nervously. They'd understood what was about to happen.

Nabbing an excellent seat beside Dorian Brooks, a gifted local poet, social activist, and fellow grandmother, I watched the 254-capacity auditorium quickly fill to overflowing: women from my yoga class, neighbors, social activists I've met over the years; more Friends scurried in, anxiously searching for an empty seat. Lynn Lazar, who'd recently had a stroke, made a grand entrance as she poled past, balanced on two thick, long, wooden dowels for support. Lynn always being Lynn, she refused my and others' offers to sit in an accessible, ground-level seat and bravely climbed the steps where, she assured us, "I'll be fine."

As someone who'd grown up moving every three years or so, I remain overjoyed whenever I bump into someone I know, even though I have now lived in the same house, a twenty-minute walk from the Yenching Auditorium, for almost forty years. So on that chilly day in March, I, too, was filled to overflowing as I watched so many people from so many parts of my life troupe past.

And as those grad students had anticipated, their polite, diffident usher role soon morphed into stern bouncer: "No, you can't save that seat; people are still waiting outside." And, "No, you can't sit there; that's a fire hazard." As a Harvard dean admitted in his introductory remarks, "If we'd known so many people would show up, we would have booked the

[Harvard-owned] Sanders Theater." Which seats over a thousand people.

Over the years, I have attended many readings and panel discussions and lectures featuring beloved authors to discover that sometimes a writer whose work I've admired can be less than godlike in real life. When a teenager and living in Lynchburg, for example, one evening my mother and I drove to nearby Sweet Briar College for a reading by Robert Frost. He'd stopped, mid-recitation, to scold a young woman seated in the second row who'd been knitting. Did my mother, a knitter, herself, criticize Frost's public shaming on the drive home? I'd like to think she did. Looking back, now, though, I also wonder if the aging poet might have briefly forgotten a line—and needed someone to blame.

I'd loved hearing about Powers's decision to live near the ancient trees of the Smokies; I'd instantly connected with Robin Wall Kimmerer, who proved to be, as I noted in my journal, the real deal who spoke with hope yet with tears in her voice. She spoke to me; she spoke to my soul. And having taken in her and Powers's and Tempest Williams's moving and telling words describing a complicated and wondrous world in which humans are not at its center, I am now, as if holding Lynn's sturdy dowels, one wooden rod in each grateful hand, steadied and buoyed, my reverent feet squarely planted on Mother Earth.

This I know experientially: there is something deeply ironic and strange and a little ridiculous about my—and thousands of others'—conversion to this growing, anti-anthropocentric understanding because we'd all read the same bestsellers. *(Sweetgrass,* published in 2013, would become a bestseller in 2020, an unusual feat in the publishing world.)

Shouldn't I have sensed that the birch trees right outside my meetinghouse window had much to teach me if, in the silence of Sunday morning worship, I would only listen? With great sadness and greater humility, I must acknowledge that, a descendent of British colonists who'd firmly believed in The Doctrine of Discovery,[36] I had been so inculcated by the dominant, Western, Christian society I was born into that I never knew different or better.

But, as that SRO crowd at the Yenching Auditorium made clear, something is happening, shifting.

**

In the summer of 2019, when getting on an airplane to visit a grandchild was carbon-footprint-problematic but possible, my husband and I flew to Duluth, Minnesota, our first trip to that part of the world, to see our two-year-old granddaughter, Amy, and her parents. Renting a wonderful, art-filled house on Park Point, a narrow spit of land adjoining downtown Duluth and jutting into Lake Superior, we'd appreciated being within walking distance of the world's largest freshwater lake. When not spending precious time with family, we walked along the oceanic-like Park Point beach; we drove up Route 61 to explore that "No salt, no sharks, no worries" lake's lighthouses. I even swam in Superior's icy water. Efficiently!

One afternoon, at the recommendation of our rental's owner, Pat Burns, who is herself a painter and serves on the advisory board of the Tweed Museum, we visited that delightful museum, housed on the University of Minnesota campus. *Intersections*, featuring contemporary artworks by nineteen Great Lakes-based Indigenous artists, was on display. The very first painting I saw, "Creation Story," by Rabbett Before Horses Strickland,[37] raised the hairs on the back of my neck.

I know this story, I realized. It's like the story that begins *Braiding Sweetgrass*.

For there was the partially raised back of Turtle. There was Otter; there was plucky Muskrat—the sacrificial hero of the story. (Just as Thomas Wazhashk, his last name the Ojibwe word for "muskrat," is the hero of Indigenous writer Louise Erdrich's wonderful *The Night Watchman*.) In Strickland's painting, the Skywoman of Kimmerer's telling has been replaced by Nanabozho, the Ojibwe shape-shifting, rabbit-eared trickster often found at the center of his amazing work. I stood, entranced, delighted to be able to connect with the ancient tale depicted.

Sadly, much of the art I walked past and admired that afternoon I'd only appreciated thinly. How little I knew and know of the depth, the backstories, the legends and traditions informing the nineteen Native artists represented at the Tweed's exhibit. But I did recognize something in Strickland's painting: I know the blue background surrounding Turtle Island. I know that blue. It's the blue sky of this latitude. It's the blue above Lake Superior. It's the blue that humans who have inhabited this bit of Turtle Island have known for eons. Since Skywoman fell out of the sky.

In that moment, did it matter that the painting before me features Nanabozho rather than Skywoman? No, it didn't. Why? Because, I think, it was a story I recognized—a creation story in which Muskrat must die for life to begin—a redemptive tale so much more appealing to me than the Genesis story.

This is ensemble storytelling; this is wholeness; this creation story is far more than the sum of its characters. Precisely as Strickland tells it, wholeness huddles together on Turtle Island: animals, shape-shifting deity, wet earth. Whoever plays the inbreaking role, be it Skywoman or Nanabozho, doesn't matter. What matters is that pregnant moment the artist depicts, when the precious mud Muskrat brought to the surface from the depths of the water surrounding Turtle Island is first released from rabbit-eared Nanabozho's human-shaped hand.

In Kimmerer's version, when Skywoman first toppled, she'd grabbed at the Tree of Life as she fell and so, clutched in her hand, were the seeds and fruits she brought with her. Using Muskrat's mud, the sun shining through the hole she'd tumbled through, Skywoman dances—and turns Turtle Island green.

And everything changed.

Jewish and Christian traditions tell inbreaking stories—of astonishing moments when something breaks through, like an inexplicable burning bush or a strange and wondrous star to announce the birth of baby born in a stable. And everything changes. For seventeenth-century George Fox, that something was the prophetic voice he discovered, over and over, in his well-read Bible; he'd recognized God's inbreaking in David, in Isaiah, and, of course, in Jesus.

"Fox certainly in his early period when he was breaking his way with dynamic effect, was the bearer of this great faith that God and man in his inmost depth are asundered.... This glowing insight of Fox champions the faith that at our highest and best and truest attainment of life, we reveal the fact of something infinite and transcendent breaking through our finite lives. We discover the eternal in the midst of our temporal lives," Jones notes.[38]

"Christ is come to teach his people himself," Fox preached. Present tense. Here and now, that which is God/All/Wholeness/Light is present, with us, within us, and like the Life-filled birdsong from the scruffiest, dustiest sparrow, like the deep wisdom of the birch trees outside the meetinghouse, always available.

**

Sometimes nature means open and unpeopled and wild—a place I drive to or, like Lake Superior, travel by airplane so as to marvel. Sometimes, in these days of COVID-19, yearning to lose myself in the beauty and majesty surrounding me, I drive to a nearby wildlife preserve or refuge and, masked and filled with wonder and joy, I gratefully walk through a magnificent forest or beside a pristine kettle pond.

But sometimes, especially during this first spring during lockdown when, as my friend Minga Claggett-Borne noted, "Death is all around us and spring has never been so amazing," I sit on my back deck and listen to this tiny piece of real estate's abundance of birds.

In 2012, the City of Somerville created a small, delightfully landscaped park from a vacant lot on Quincy Street, the next street over; this lot abuts our carriage house. (After the park had opened but before the city hooked up a water supply, my husband and I watered its tender plantings with our own hose.) Definitely operating from a shared sense of scarcity, when this possible green space had been first proposed, the initial neighborhood meetings at City Hall were contentious. One night, neighbors yelling and interrupting each other, an off-duty police officer seated amongst us jested *sotto voce*—but loud enough for me to hear, "Shoulda brought my gun." Eventually, as if coached by our neighborhood's flora and fauna, who do not recognize fences or property rights, we bickerers found common ground. So, now my husband's and my tenth-of-an-acre lot, sizeable by Somerville standards, is part of a larger, bird-rich eco-system.

Seated on my deck, drinking my morning coffee, and writing in my journal, I am surrounded by birdsong. Cardinals, blue jays, sparrows, house finches, chickadees, goldfinches (in Ojibwe, goldfinches are "leaf counters," a fun-fact I'd learned at the Tweed Museum), robins, the ever-performing neighborhood mockingbird—three swallows circle like Lynn's right hand.

And I am filled with—is there a noun for this?—that feeling Minga described of "never been so"; I have never felt such deep gratitude shrouded by such deep sadness.

**

Sometimes nature lies beyond my backyard but still very close to home. On my masked walks through Somerville these days, hungry for a glimpse of Turtle Island green, I've noticed inexplicably tall pine trees towering over the two- or three-story frame houses beside them, their needled branches filling what little remains of a city plot. Those pine trees are all over the city. Why weren't these giants cut down years ago? How have these magnificent trees survived in a formerly working-class city where landscaping could sometimes mean a postage-stamp-sized, asphalt-sealed yard dotted by one or two joint-compound buckets filled with plastic flowers?

(To be fair, even in the "Bad Old Days" when this city had been labeled *Slummerville,* some homeowners, many of them Italian or Portuguese, tended grape arbors or one or two fruit trees; they'd farmed compact, often terraced gardens. And if those aging homeowners have not been priced out of their homes, they still do.)

Had these pine trees survived because they look like three-story Christmas trees and were therefore holy? Are they still here because they don't require leaf-raking or the yearly, dangerous ritual of unclogging the gutters? Or do they remain because, for generations, the human occupants of Somerville's tiny plots have loved to fall asleep, windows open, and listen to the sound of wind soughing through pine branches? As humans have loved that same soothing sound since Skywoman fell out of the sky and Jesus walked this precious Earth? I don't know. But I am childishly grateful whenever I spot one.

"Fewer birds sing just as loud," Veronica Barron, a young woman from my meeting offered at a recent Zoom meeting for worship as she'd sat outside in her own tiny backyard. Sparrows and crows, maybe a pigeon or two audible in the background, I heard so much in her message: I heard her pain at nature's diminishment. I heard her joy to be in worship in citified nature. I heard her celebrate robust aliveness; I heard her radical acceptance of what is here, available, now. As is. And sacred.

**

Now we must add my grandchildren's twisted, braided flowers and birds, maybe even a tiny turtle or wobbly birch tree, to our hair wreath. Human hair is much harder to work with than Play-Doh or clay or beeswax. We may not recognize what these six children create. It doesn't matter.

Three-alarm fire, Quincy Street,
Somerville, Massachusetts, May 20, 2020.

Just like Your Mother

A true story with a few important details removed: in about 1989, a dear friend did something unforgivable—or so it seemed at the time. Furious when I learned what she'd done, I'd paced back and forth, back and forth, in my bedroom, cursing, crying, hands clenched. At one point, I remember, I'd looked down at those clenched fists as if not mine: "Whoa!" I realized. "I look like Carrie on prom night but without the blood!"

That same night, there had been a terrible fire in my (ex) friend's building, and she'd been forced to move.

Another, related story with more details: ten years earlier, I'd discovered that an ancestor, Abigail Dane Faulkner, had been accused of witchcraft in 1692, but according to a handwritten family history I'd unearthed, she'd been "acquitted for her piety." Doubting this bit of family lore, I began to research the Salem witchcraft trials. In a huge, leather-bound book housed at the Boston Public Library, I found my ancestor's trial transcript that I was allowed to photocopy, page by page, leaving a snow flurry of white paper on the BPL floor from wherever my fingers or the copier made contact with that precious book. (I should never have been allowed to even open it!)

As I'd suspected, Abigail Dane Faulkner had not been acquitted for her piety. In fact, at her trial, she'd argued against "spectral evidence"; that even if witnesses claimed her shape had harmed them, she, Abigail, had never consented to anything her accusers claimed she'd done. She and her shape were two different things, she'd reasoned. She'd cursed the judge, too!

Found guilty, my feisty ancestor's hanging was postponed because she'd been pregnant. She'd signed *The Devil's Book*, it was assumed—her unborn baby had not. According to the English law of that time, a pregnant woman's hanging must wait until after she'd given birth. By the time that baby was born, however, her accusers had recanted, and Abigail Dane Faulkner was released, baby boy in arms. My family's branch of the Faulkner family is descended from that jail-born child.

Back home in Wethersfield, Connecticut, and seated at my desk one summer morning, I'd been transcribing that copied trial account when, just as I copied out my furious ancestor's curse, "I wish you ill," there was a simultaneous phosphorous-bright flash and tremendous crash! Lightning had struck the house next door. Terrified, I dove under my desk.

I do not believe my clenched, "Carrie" fists hurled fire bolts across Somerville and set my ex-friend's house on fire. (It was later rumored a careless tenant had.) I do not believe a three-hundred-year-old curse possesses diabolical powers any more than I believe in spectral evidence.

And yet: an emergent mystic, I am intrigued by my friend Kevin Thomas's declaration: "There are no coincidences." A part of myself I only dimly understand senses that, as he so often is, Kevin might be right. So when recalling these incendiary events, I chose to stay in a confounded and paradoxical place of humbly and respectfully knowing and not knowing. And to remain awed. Yes. Always.

I know this, though: I have been justifiably afraid of my own negative energy, my own anger—the same anger, in differing amounts, I have nevertheless directed at others. I have terrified my daughters. I have infuriated two ex-husbands. Once, years ago, standing on a Manhattan street corner, I so fiercely blasted a cab driver that he'd slumped and shrugged his shoulders as he slowly drove away. In the recent past, I completely lost it with someone at my Quaker meeting. Twice! After the second ugly scene, as I have already mentioned, I'd shamefully talked about these encounters with my Nurturing Faithfulness Group—and began to examine my anger. Finally.

In my family, sadness was strongly discouraged, but anger was not. We four witnessed our parents getting angry at each other; we knew and accepted that their spats were as much a part of our family life as dinner promptly at six. We also knew when it was about to get ugly. "You're just like your father," my mother would hiss. "You're just like your mother!" Dad would snap, his voice raised.

Time to leave the room!

Our family's normality around anger had been unusual—or so I came to understand after later comparing notes with friends. Just as, in my twenties, I'd discovered after talking with other fledgling feminists that, when I was ten or eleven, my mother's starry-eyed and breathless bedtime revelation that "sex is a beautiful and wonderful thing" had not been a universally shared mother-daughter chat.

I can only speculate that, given my mother's fatherless childhood and the enormous disparity between our Radcliffe-educated grandma and our intellectually disabled grandpa—"Why did she ever marry him?" my grandmother's sister once asked my father—when it came to gender roles and anger, our parents, lacking traditional role models, were curiously egalitarian. That blue and white coaster, always just there on the living room's coffee table of whatever house we'd lived in, a ceramic square declaring, "What's sauce for the goose is sauce for the gander," had applied to my parents' gender equality around anger, too.

**

In fifth or sixth grade, I'd come home from school one day to discover all my bureau drawers emptied, their contents piled high on my bed and the now-empty drawers a tottering tower stacked beside my bureau. On my bureau was an angry note saying how disgusted my mother had been when, putting away clean laundry, she'd discovered my just-tossed-into-drawers messiness.

She hadn't laid a finger on me. In no way had my mother physically hurt me. I bear no visible scars. Yet there, piled on my bed and stacked against my bureau, was painful evidence of domestic violence in the very specific yet universal sense that, like all domestic violence, the perpetrator is someone who supposedly loves you yet causes you harm.

What kind of mother does what my mother had done? Infuriated ten- or eleven-year-old me knew: the kind of mother who, too, must be assaulted, violated, punished—without my laying a finger on her, either. So I removed a nine-by-twelve, black-and-white studio photograph of my mother from its frame and, with a straight pin, furiously stabbed holes all over my mother's lovely face before putting it back on my bedroom wall where it remained, seemingly untouched.

Had I found that act satisfying? Yes.

I know my mother later found that desecrated photograph. I know she'd confronted me. I know I'd confessed. I know Mom merely nodded but said nothing. I know how I'd interpreted that nod; my mother's silence meant acceptance. What I don't know is when this mother-daughter conversation happened. How old would I have been when I first learned that rage is okay?

My fuzziness points to those four confusing years when our family found ourselves living on the west bank of the James River in the Jim Crow city of Lynchburg, Virginia. Each of us reacted to that move differently; we took turns being off-kilter. Out of focus. Confused. So probably sometime between the ages of fourteen and eighteen as Mom chauffeured me somewhere—on the drive home from the Robert Frost reading, perhaps—I'd absorbed a lesson on rage that confused and hindered me for years.

But I realize now, during that fraught time, I'd received other lessons on long-held anger and rage. For the Wilds had arrived in Lynchburg in 1959, just as the Civil Rights movement began to unfold. My anger instructors, whose quiet, staid hometown had just been invaded by "tacky Yankees" and whose carefully delineated "separate but equal" status quo was being challenged by multiple lawsuits, had been classmates, my high school teachers, neighbors. I observed how a careless word caused residual anger, passed on from generation to generation, to suddenly erupt. "Civil? Civil? There was nothing civil about it," a classmate shouted at me my first day of E.C. Glass High School. "It was 'The War of Northern Aggression', and don't you forget it!" I witnessed how my male classmates—inwardly seething, I see this, now—were cruel and mean-spirited and openly racist—and no one intervened. Like my mother when she'd dumped my stuff, like me when I retaliated, my Lynchburg-based teachers had been furious. And none of us knew how to manage such powerful emotions.

Powerful emotions—and more complicated than I'd understood at fifteen: "The South will rise again," those teenage boys would threaten my breasts—even though the presence of a buxom and affluent Yankee standing right in front of them might have raised doubts about that prediction. All these years later, to be reminded of those adolescent encounters (and what I wished I'd said back then: "Up here, bub! My face is actually up here!") is, mysteriously, to be reminded of my sister's reminder: "Look for shame. It may be attached to something else." The South lost that bloody, bloody war, be it *civil* or not.

**

I know exactly where my father and I had been when, after another heated argument with my mother, he sat me down to set me straight. Again. We'd been in our four-bedroom split-level in Lynchburg. My gawky portrait monitoring our conversation, Dad and I sat in the living room in front of the window facing our neglected backyard and its lonely swingset. Visible beyond our property line were the spacious pastures of the Presbyterian Orphan Home's farm. Sometimes, I remember, my bedroom window open, I'd fall asleep listening to the deep, mournful bellow of the farm's bull. (One of my unhoused students had grown up in that orphanage.)

At fifteen, I knew these father-daughter sessions would go on and on; to interrupt was strictly forbidden, and most important, at some unexpected moment, my father would stop his rant to ask a random question just to make sure I was still listening. (He'd picked up this sly technique when he'd been in sales.) This Dad lecture would end after my mumbled and contrite response to his, "And what have you learned from this experience?"

This time, however, it was my father who learned something. For, to my astonishment, he'd begged me to be more sympathetic to my mother because she had her period. And then explained what, every month, my mother experienced.

"Yeah, I know," I interrupted. I couldn't help myself. "The same thing happens to me every month!" I didn't say out loud, "And you don't see me demanding that all normal life in this family cease, do you?" My indignant tone said it all.

He'd blinked. He'd taken this in. But continued to blame Mom's period for her outsized anger.

The part of me looking at my own outsized anger wishes my father, having gained some further understanding of menstruation based on my experience, had intervened, put his foot down, stopped enabling. Had that happened, I wonder, might I have learned something about anger and proportionality? Might I, growing up in such a wished-for household, have come to understand that, yes, in the face of injustice or microaggressions or outright cruelty, anger is acceptable and justifiable—but over-the-top fury is not okay?

Another part of me is appalled by this childish and longed-for narrative in which the family patriarch defines what is and isn't acceptable behavior; the storied *Father Knows Best* dad who steps in and, once again, saves the day.

Had my mother been taught by her mother that, for one week every month, all women are powerless to control themselves? Had my mother believed that over-the-top behavior to be her monthly, biological imperative? Is that what her mother taught her? Had Lil learned this from her mother, also a Lillian? Had, indeed, my mother been just like her mother?

What had any of my forebears been taught about their own body's hormonal changes? Lil claimed that, when she'd attended her fancy finishing school, she'd been taught how to pour tea. That's it. Her finishing school training to become some wealthy man's wife meant, when divorced with two young daughters, that working in the Bridgeport Hospital kitchen had been her only option. "When I think of my mother, I think of the burn scars on her hands," my mother told me once. What did my scarred and poorly educated grandmother understand about her own body?

I'm reminded of a story I heard almost fifty years ago when, for three years, I'd taught at the American School for the Deaf in West Harford, Connecticut. Most students lived at the school during the school week and returned home on the weekends; this story happened on a Monday morning. One of my colleagues reported that one of his best and brightest high school students had come to class that morning, slammed her books on her desk, refused to work, picked fights with her classmates, acted out. So he'd invited her to meet with him after class, and after some careful, patient, gentle probing, not unlike the evoking questions of a Nurturing Faithfulness meeting, I'm guessing, he discovered she'd recently begun to menstruate. Male, new to working with adolescents, he'd felt out of his depth, but as he later explained, her personality change had been so dramatic, he was pretty sure something else was going on, something he might be able to help with. More careful questioning, and he discovered the source of this stellar student's uncharacteristic rage: like many hearing parents of deaf children in those days (I assume this has changed), this deaf student's mother only knew a few words of American Sign Language (ASL). So the previous weekend, the student's mother inadvertently used the sign for months, as in, "Your period will last five or six months," instead of days.

No wonder that young woman was furious! (Given her mother's poor sign language skills, what other misinformation had her daughter received?) Why wouldn't that deaf student feel angry and helpless that this mysterious thing happened to her? For months? How deeply unfair! Of course she'd thrown her books on her desk! Of course!

What have I learned from this experience? Whenever I'd erupted with ex-husband number two, his response would invariably be: "Aren't you about to get your period?" I'd sputter. I'd deny. He'd always been right. So I admit with genuine contrition that my surging hormones contributed to those explosions. That our marriage was in deep trouble certainly contributed, too. But that my amp had been cranked up to eleven? I own that. Had I been able to dispassionately talk about the ways our relationship needed help, could my ex-husband have heard me? I think so. I mourn those forever-lost opportunities and what those losses have meant for our daughters.

Having failed at marriage—twice—I believed I'd forever disqualified myself to love and to be loved ever again. Isn't that how the universe works? Wasn't that fair? Supported, held by another group of Quaker women, my single parent group, I saw myself growing older with them; I imagined we'd all buy a big, shabby, rambling house together someday, maybe in western Massachusetts, and take care of one another when we got old and frail. We'd grow old together.

But in 1992, I was, like C.S. Lewis, "surprised by joy" when I met a quiet, gentle man at a weekend retreat my meeting hosted. After a couple of dates with the wonderful man I have now been married to for the past twenty-five years, I shared my ambivalence with my single parent group. "I don't know," I confessed. "He's not really my type."

"Yeah?" one woman pushed back. "And look how that turned out!"

The first time I erupted with Wonderful Man, he'd taken forever to respond. As the minutes ticked on and on, both of us silent, I realized: this is like worship-sharing! This is what that Quaker wedding vow, "promising with Divine Assistance to be unto you a loving and faithful wife,"actually looks like. These silences are how he and I invite Spirit into our marriage.

If I am to truly live in that virtue and power that takes away the occasion of all [conflicts],[39] which, to me, is another way to name Spirit, I should probably take a harder look at the seeds of war within me. To truly be whole, I should probably accept the parts of myself I am deeply ashamed of, too. "Wholeness does not mean perfection; it means embracing an integral part of life," Parker Palmer has noted.[40] A clumsy apprentice in this apprenticeship with grief and loss, my fledgling embrace of the ugly within me will continue to be awkward, bumpy. But it is precisely what I am being asked to do.

In a perfect world with a perfect mother, when she and I had talked about that bureau incident, something quite wonderful could have happened. Mom could have seized this opportunity, mother-to-daughter, to talk about women and anger–about the difference between justifiable anger and fury as in those terrifying, snake-coiffed Furies of Greek mythology—who, according to my fusty Bulfinch, punished those who'd "defied public justice."[41] She could have acknowledged that, yes, there's plenty of injustice to be furious about. She might have voiced how, often, life isn't fair. She might have even added, with a maternal authority I would have acknowledged and respected, "Especially, it seems, for women and children." Had she known Abigail Dane Faulkner's story, she and I could have talked about how, throughout history, angry women, outspoken women, eccentric women have been accused of being witches—and we could have shared our theories as to why.

She might have begun a sentence with, "This is no excuse but—" and speculated aloud what else in her unfulfilling suburban wife and mother-of-four life might have set her off that bureau-tossing day. Had she been worrying about one of us? Or had she just learned we were moving again because the great General Electric Company so decreed? Had her sister just called to announce she'd gotten another promotion?

Mom might have owned her own struggles around what she'd considered her female destiny: hormones and rage. She might have counseled me to, as my daughter Hope tells her daughter, "Use your words." She could have invited me to name what I'd felt, seeing my belongings dumped on my bed. Most important, she might have noted that, for both of us, our actions were all out of proportion to the other's transgression.

In a perfect world, in order to encourage me to look at my life with a wider lens and to give some space for perspective, my make-believe mom might have also pointed out that, for people of color, life is consistently not fair. She might have been moved to remind me that many impoverished ten-year-olds would be delighted to own enough underwear and socks and shirts and pajamas to fill an entire bureau—and some children could only imagine owning such a commodious piece of furniture.

My perfect mother might have told me about other mothers, who would be astonished that women like my mother, like me, could freely and without fear express an emotion those other mothers repressed, swallowed, denied, or were physically attacked for displaying. My perfect mother would have taught me that anger is a feminist issue.

So, maybe, when creating another piece for this hair-wreath-in-progress, in memory of all women, living and dead, who have been angry, who have been outraged, who have publicly raised their fists into the air or, alone and weeping, pounded their pillows, all the women who have been hung or were burned at the stake for being different or mad: out of strands of brown and black and blond and gold and flaming-red and salt-and-pepper hair, I would create something beautiful, something strong, something eruptive, volcanic, like shooting flames or writhing snakes, like a fountain or a spring welling forth. And at the base of this beautiful, multihued eruption, as if holding this creation together, in plain sight but mysterious if you don't know what they are, I would entwine the two little silver metal clasps used on a fifties sanitary napkin belt.

"Being outraged is a sure sign that our soul is awake."
Francis Weller.[77]

In a Minor Key

Maybe twenty years ago, my friend Kevin said to me, "Patricia? You know what you're like? You're like a cook on a slave ship." And I was furious! Wasn't I an ardent anti-racist? Weren't my woke credentials impeccable? Didn't I blog, again and again, about my white privilege, my cluelessness, how hard I was working on issues about race and class? Hadn't I, just a few years before Kevin said those devastating words, sung "We Shall Overcome" with Jerry Falwell in a Lynchburg church built in 1879 by newly-freed Black people? Hadn't I been led to write *Way Opens* about all of this?

But Kevin, whose ancestors had been on that slave ship, was right. It would be disingenuous—but, as Grandma would appreciate, make a good story—to claim that it has taken a global pandemic and George Floyd's murder for me to take in the truth of his words. Parts of me have always known and felt Kevin's tragic truth. But like many others living at this epochal time, my understanding of systemic racism and white supremacy has become deeper; my felt experience of systemic racism has forever shifted.

Despite my yearning to move past us/them, despite my bone-deep belief that we are all equals at the table, lies a binary I must acknowledge.

Briefly, very briefly, in the early days of this century and working on *Way Opens,* I'd sensed an opening about this essential and undeniable binary. Failing, twenty years ago, to truly look at, absorb, to take in this undeniability, I am only telling this story now.

While doing research for *Way Opens,* I'd talked with Lynchburg resident Chauncey Spencer, an early Black aviator and son of Anne Spencer, Harlem Renaissance poet. Back in Jim Crow days, Anne Spencer and her husband, Edward, hosted many notable Black people when these VIPs traveled to segregated Lynchburg; the Spencers' house guests had included Mary McLeod Bethune, Martin Luther King Jr., and Thurgood Marshall. Anne and Edward's lovely Pierce Street home and garden is now a museum and is located across the street from Dr. Robert "Whirlwind" Johnson's home—and tennis court. On that court, now gone, the Lynchburg doctor and former Lincoln University football star instructed the young Althea Gibson and Arthur Ashe.

Dazed to be in his presence, where this dashing, history-making airman and I met remains a blur; all I remember is a cool, shades-drawn, old-fashioned parlor. Interviewed many times before, almost by rote, Chauncey Spencer told me how he'd always wanted to fly; he'd taught me about the history of segregation and how, in part because of his military service and subsequent, impromptu conversation with President Harry Truman on Capitol Hill in 1948, the President enacted Executive Order No. 9981, stipulating equality of treatment and opportunity in all of the United States Armed Forces.

As this high-flying interview began its final approach, something prompted me to ask him something I had not expected to say. Maybe he'd used the phrase "color-blind" and I'd heard that phrase with fresh ears. Maybe this impulse had been a graced, inbreaking moment. Whatever the nudge, I heard myself say, "I think it's important, though, to acknowledge your experiences as a Black man growing up and living in racist America and how that has shaped you. Aren't you, in many ways, who you are because of Jim Crow?"

He'd grinned: "I never heard anyone say that before."

Chauncey Spencer bore the scars of his chained, anguished ancestors; he experienced the transgenerational trauma of his people. That trauma, passed down from generation to generation, was his family's.

Instead, this: many years ago, my mother had been hospitalized—I don't remember why—and my father, Paul, my husband, and I had gone to the hospital to visit her. Lonely and bored but recovering, Mom welcomed our company.

"You know, lying here, I've had plenty of time to think," she told us as we surrounded her bed. "I've been thinking about the racial situation and how little I've done. I didn't do enough." (Understanding, now, that her seemingly random comments were usually precipitated by something, I suspect she'd been prompted to consider our nation's grim history because several of the hospital staff had been people of color.)

"You marched in Selma!" one of us pointed out. And she had. After GE moved our family from Lynchburg to Huntsville, Alabama, in 1964, my mother joined with others from Huntsville's Unitarian Universalist church on that historic civil rights march.

"Yes, I know," she replied mournfully. "But I didn't die!"

The four of us laughed so hard a nurse scurried into Mom's room to tell us to please be quiet!

We'd snickered at Mom's guilt because we didn't want to deal with the painful history she'd acknowledged or our own resultant feelings. Sacrificing her life for civil rights seemed ridiculously disproportionate—wasn't it? We snickered because we didn't know. We'd snickered because we could.

What else can we do? Stroll into any store, any bank, any hotel lobby, any restaurant, any upscale, leafy neighborhood without incident. My family carries its privilege wherever we go.

More than twenty years ago, my Quaker meeting, moved by the writings of Peggy McIntosh and Tim Wise,[42] conducted a series of workshops on white privilege. (Long after those workshops ended, I continued to carry one workshop handout, Kenneth Jones and Tema Okun's "White Supremacy Culture,"[43] in my shoulder bag "lest I forget.") A couple of times in my earliest days of understanding how racialized America actually functions, I used my newly minted (yet still partial) understanding of white privilege "for good."

The first time, another white woman and I had been canvassing for Pat Jehlen, a white, progressive candidate running for state senator. Pounding the pavement, my canvass buddy and I were briefly stymied when we discovered that, to enter an apartment building in Medford Square, we'd needed to either know the building's security code or to be buzzed in. Or, I realized, to be white. "White privilege," I muttered to my compatriot as I grabbed the front door when someone had exited. Sure enough, no one stopped us. (Pat won and is still a dedicated, hard-working, much-needed voice on Beacon Hill.)

In 2006, awaiting the birth of my first grandchild, I'd cleared my June calendar so as to be available when needed. So, I realized one morning, I could show up at a racial profiling case happening that week at Cambridge District Court. The defendants, Calvin Belfon and Isiah Anderson, were Black teenagers who, at a street carnival, had been involved in a nasty confrontation with the Medford police. Most of the spectators in that Cambridge courtroom were Black; all but one of the jury was white. "Okay," I thought, "if I'm to be a conspicuous white person in support of these kids, maybe I should embrace my 'white supremacy culture.'" Remembering one of Jones's and Okun's most depressingly true tenets, "worship of the written word," I'd pulled out a pen and notebook from my shoulder bag and began taking notes. Conspicuously. "Thank you for being here," one of the defense lawyers told me during a break. "You're making a difference."

A news article reported that "Belfon was found not guilty of five assault and battery charges but guilty of disorderly conduct and resisting arrest. Anderson was found not guilty of seven charges that included assault and battery but guilty of two charges of assault and battery and one each of disorderly conduct and resisting arrest. Both were sentenced to two years' probation and some community service; Belfon credited community support that he and his co-defendant had not faced jail time."[44]

Telling these decades-old stories may seem like virtue-signaling; my intention is to make clear that, like the fictive cook ladling out extra portions when safe to do so, in the earliest days of this century, this is what Kevin's slave ship had looked like.

In 2020 I read everything I could about COVID-19 and, horrified by this virus's insidious, adaptive brilliance, had been terrified and exhausted all the time. Termed "high risk" at my age, I was sure every cough, every ache meant I was going to die. And because I had not yet learned how much additional energy and self-care nonstop anxiety requires, any additional stress to my normal routine exhausted me. The first Sunday I'd facilitated a virtual forum, a forty-five minute venue at my Quaker meeting usually attended by thirty-five to forty people, I'd been so nervous to use Zoom, a technology I was not yet comfortable with, that the minute I'd clicked "Leave Meeting," I began to sweat and shake. (Ever needing to be the gracious hostess, that our presenter that morning, Dr. Abraham Sussman, a noted psychotherapist and Sufi practitioner, had not been someone from my meeting, added to my stress.) Dizzy and terrified, angry we had a lifetime supply of adhesive bandages in our medicine cabinet but no thermometer, I crawled into bed and slept for the rest of the day.

Months later, alive and healthy, I realized that "high risk" requires a couple of asterisks:

*Affluent older people who have received excellent health care their entire lives are far less at risk.

*Those who can radically reduce their interactions with others, like not being dependent on public transportation or who can afford to pay extra to buy whatever they need online, are far less at risk.

Greater Boston nursing home and grocery store workers, many of them people of color, began dying from the virus. These fatalities, reported in *The Boston Globe*, were real people for me; I'd interacted with actual men and women who performed those underpaid, often thankless, frontline jobs. I'd known Edith and Alfred, who'd lovingly and patiently cared for my mother at Neville Center. (It had been Alfred who'd called to tell me my mother had died.) And although many of them I only knew as names embossed on a plastic nametag, I'd had nodding, pleasant, and often daily interactions with the employees of my neighborhood's discount supermarket, Market Basket, half a block away. Ana, Timmy, Marissa, Mike, Tanya, Johnny; for me, these frontline workers weren't an abstraction or a catch-all descriptive; some, like Johnny, the stand-up comic of the deli department, lived in my neighborhood. So when I read "frontline" in *The Globe*, I could supply faces, smiles, names, the conversations I'd had with Alfred or Edith or Johnny or Joe Amaral, Market Basket's warm, hard-working manager. Some in their teens and working for the first time, frontline workers performed their jobs with dignity and with humor but with little choice. I worked from home.

 In April of 2020, densely populated Chelsea, home to thousands of low-income Spanish-speaking families and located directly across the Mystic River from Boston, became a hot spot. As my husband and I discovered in the fall of 2019, when we'd attended an Actors Shakespeare Project's innovative performance of *King Lear* in a tiny Chelsea theater, that impoverished city lay directly beneath Logan Airport's approach. Briefly, mercifully briefly, my husband and I experienced what it is like to be poor and forced to live beneath Logan's relentless traffic—and to breathe Chelsea's abysmal air. This environmental justice issue in an "affordable" greater Boston community has directly impacted Chelsea's hot spot status. I live elsewhere. As Lear would rage: "O cruel! O ye gods!"

During this fraught, cruel time, my friends and I sent our stimulus check money to food banks and shelters. Like my fossil-fuels voluntary tax group, we'd mailed checks to aid undocumented and now unemployed workers and their families. Every evening, some of us banged on pots and pans to express our gratitude for frontline workers. We curbside-shopped local. Some of us drove in caravans and circled Massachusetts prisons on behalf of those behind bars in grave danger from this virus. But although every week my friend, Minga, helped to sort donations at a food pantry in a Chelsea church basement, most of my friends, like me, stayed safely home.

Quarantined, my busy, distracting life on hold, I watched countless people of color deliver packages to me and my neighbors: our mail, the take-out dinners from the Indian restaurant in Union Square, the delivery of my new sneakers, that copy of *Daddy-Long-Legs* I'd ordered from Alibris.com, the thermometer we late-to-the-party ordered, or the ingredients we'd needed to make our own hand sanitizer. This neighborhood's blissful quiet, how serene it suddenly became when Union Square construction projects halted? When, because of the shutdown, the daily, nonstop motorcade of pickups and panel trucks and noisy tractor-trailers ceased? How the wildlife of this urban ecosystem—birds in particular—emboldened by this quiet, came closer? My God, I realized, one day, when a robin on a neighbor's chain-link fence let me share a little patch of sidewalk space, this serenity comes at the price of those construction worker's jobs. Many of them from El Salvador and Guatemala and Brazil.

I am a person of privilege. I cannot swerve nor veer from what Kevin said about me being a cook on a slave ship.

**

God gave Moses the rainbow sign
No more water, but fire next time[45]

I'd been living in Wethersfield when I first learned of the Order of the Occult Hand. Every year, *The Hartford Courant*, the Nutmeg State's primary newspaper, publishes the names of the Order's latest inductees, journalists from all over the country who'd somehow managed to slip the purple-prose phrase, "It was as if an occult hand had—" past their no-nonsense copy editors. Those yearly articles were fascinating reading—both to appreciate those newly inducted members' moxie and to discover what improbable or inexplicable or eerie events deserved such raised-eyebrows language.

I do not believe some occult hand has created COVID-19. Nor do I believe an occult hand perfectly positioned Darnella Frazier, the young Black woman who videoed George Floyd's murder, to stand exactly where she stood. But since this pandemic began, I have found myself wondering: Are we living in a time of Biblical-proportion inbreaking? For my twenty-first century, science-based understanding of how the universe works does not preclude me from sometimes imagining that proverbial occult hand—or maybe that capricious trickster, Nanabozho—has again swooped down to Earth to interfere, disrupt, change everything. I may have learned in sixth grade what causes a rainbow, but I am still irrationally comforted to spot such improbable brilliance spanning the horizon. And grateful to again be reminded of God's storied promise.

But I am also capable of irrational fear: on the same evening more COVID-19 cases had been reported to the World Health Organization in the previous twenty-four hours than ever before [May 20, 2020], a three-alarm fire broke out in a two-family house on Quincy Street—the next street over from my house—terrifyingly close. Fire trucks' flashing lights illuminated the billowing smoke filling our neighborhood as I stood on my front porch, my apocalyptic street unrecognizable. "We're being punished," I thought. "Life as we know it has ended. We're doomed."

But in the light of day, when I calmly began to examine my very human reaction, I saw how occult-hand-blaming is much like my anger-for-sadness. For many of us in hard times, blame is our go-to, automatic reaction; it's what we humans do.

We blame an occult hand or capricious, mischievous gods; we blame one another, too. In March of 2020, soon after shelter-in-place and social distancing protocols went into effect in Massachusetts, I saw what the current face of blame looks like—and it's ugly. On the same day the president of the United States called the coronavirus "the Chinese virus," I bumped into a former student I'd known when I'd worked as a counselor at Somerville's adult education center. Warmly dressed, this former student, probably my age, had been waiting in a bus shelter in Porter Square. So I stopped and, keeping the required six-foot distance, called out their name.

"Oh, hi," they replied without much energy or warmth. Their enervation, I surmised, was related to COVID-19 so, after first asking if they were okay and safe, said something about the current situation.

"The virus?" they asked; their accent flavoring their terse words. I nodded.

"Ya know," they said, leaning forward with a we-both-know-what's-really-going-on look. And rubbed their thumb and forefinger together, the universal sign for money. Their narrowed eyes and conspiratorial face, those rubbing fingers; I knew where this conversation was headed.

"I'm not listening to this," I told them, turning on my heels.

"God bless you," they called after me.

I did not feel blessed.

Stewing, brooding, I stomped home. Who, I wondered, did they believe profited from this pandemic? The Chinese government? Big Pharma? Dr. Fauci? Given what crossed their face when they'd rubbed their fingers together, to name a particular scapegoat—and there will always be scapegoats—probably doesn't matter. What matters is the ugliness I observed at a six-foot distance, not as a black-and-white photograph of, say, leering, angry, white teenagers pouring ketchup on sit-in protesters at a Jackson, Mississippi, drugstore counter in 1963 but right in front of me. On the face of someone I know. A neighbor. There it was. There it is. A real-time glimpse of hatred.

Descendent of an accused witch, I do not excuse scapegoating. Nor do I shake my fist at a malevolent, occult hand. But I do blame; oh, yes. I blame the present-day humans who have by their inaction or willful action needlessly propagated this virus. I am angry—justifiably angry at them. Furious as in those super-pissed Furies angered by those who would defy public justice. My anger is tempered by abiding, deep, profound sadness at the enormity of suffering this pandemic has wreaked. And trust that, as it had done many times before this apprenticeship, my anger will fuel Something.

**

Where is Spirit in all of this? When the pandemic's global impact first took hold, my friend, Chris Jorgenson, had been in Palestine, working with students and staff at the Ramallah Friends School on a short-term landscaping and tree-planting project. Because of the pandemic, however, Chris was told she had to return to the States. Deeply disappointed not to be able to finish an exciting project she and the others had begun, she'd sought Spirit's guidance: "What does this mean? What am I being asked to understand? What am I asked to do?"

What came to Chris, living and working in occupied Palestinian territory, with its checkpoints and roadblocks and apartheid, with its arbitrary and randomly cruel, day-to-day hardships, was about living with uncertainty.

When Chris shared this insight at a recent forum, I was moved both that she'd been living in occupied Palestinian territory when this understanding came to her—from my occasional prison visits, I've learned a little something about arbitrary and randomly cruel interactions in an oppressive environment—and how, by pronouncing that one word, she'd encapsulated so much of my own anxious, scrambling, confounding experience of, as my friend, Ann Foster, put it, "Covid Spring."

How useful it is, in times like these, to be able to name the situation. Labeling this pandemic-centered, hapless, confusing, terrifying, quick-changing situation as uncertainty doesn't lessen or change or overcome all we're experiencing; cascading feelings—"rainbow feelings," my granddaughter, Lilian, would say. But to be able to recognize what's unfolding, to identify it, to say out loud, "Oh, this again?" offers some agency, I've discovered.

As "Covid Spring" moved into "Covid Summer," I began to recognize something about these uncertain times—déjà vu all over again. But how could that be? Having decided to avoid crowded, narrow-aisles Market Basket and seriously limit how often we food-shopped, for example, my husband and I began to shop once a week at a tiny, locally sourced grocery store, Neighborhood Produce, a quarter-mile walk from our house. (It goes without saying, but I will say it anyway: yes, privileged again, we could afford to pay that locally sourced store's prices.) Never quite certain from week to week what Neighborhood Produce might have in stock, we stretched out whatever we'd been able to buy for as long as possible. Why did such forbearance feel so familiar?

Gradually, it came to me: born a year before World War II ended, raised by parents who'd endured the Depression and the privations of wartime, my earliest years had been all about stretching out, making do, doing without, "Is this trip necessary?" No wonder I'd recognized such cheese-paring! To feel such kinship, such appreciation, such gratitude for Mom and Dad, to reconnect with their spirit of positivity and their "We're all in this together" energy? What a grace-rich, in-breaking blessing!

A harsh teacher, this pandemic asks us to adapt, to learn to live with nonstop uncertainty, to be nonstop uncomfortable. We're at an "After the Red Sea" but before "The Promised Land" epochal moment. We're asked to remain open. And, always, to "Let us then try what Love will do."[46]

**

After George Floyd's murder on Monday, May 25, 2020, local activists organized a stand-in in Porter Square for the following Sunday morning. Which happened to be Pentecost. My soul yearning to be in community with all those who shared my horror at both Floyd's murder and the many deaths of so many people of color by the police, mindful of all the actions I'd skipped and all the demonstrations I'd said no to during "Covid Spring," I wanted to go. But after months of cosseted quarantine, I had considerable agoraphobia and considerable inertia to overcome. So I'd wavered. Trusting Spirit, I went to bed believing I'd wake up knowing what to do.

The next morning, although still reluctant, I was clear that I should go. "You can walk there and back," I coached my hesitant self. "No public transportation required. And you don't have to worry about smashing into the other cars of a car-procession protest. Go!" So I magic-markered a sign from one of the large cardboard boxes delivered to my home; "Say their names: George Floyd, Breanna Taylor, Ahmaud Arbury."

On a propitious, spectacular, early summer Sunday, I joined maybe fifty, maybe a hundred protesters, most of us white, most of us over sixty, who stood at six-foot intervals on either side of Massachusetts Avenue in Porter Square near the T. "Black Lives Matter" signs held high, we waved, and street traffic honked. It was lovely and peaceful. I was filled.

Was I filled by that early summer sun on my taut shoulders? That, indeed, I was in community? And safe? Yes. But filled, too, by the same fiery spirit that Pentecost commemorates—that moment, seven Sundays after Easter when, according to Acts 2, the apostles were gathered in one place, "When suddenly there came from the sky a noise like that of a strong driving wind, which filled the whole house where they were sitting. And there appeared to them tongues like flames of fire dispersed among them and resting on each one. And they were all filled with the Holy Spirit and began to talk in other tongues, as the Spirit gave them power of utterance."

(As I transcribe this Bible passage, I see Reverend Owen Cardwell Jr. on a Sunday morning in Richmond, Virginia. Dressed in his white vestments, he stands at the New Canaan International Church's pulpit, "Help me, Holy Ghost!" I hear him beseech.)

Had the stand-in's organizers picked that particular, foundational Sunday in the Christian calendar to stage that demonstration? Probably not. I'm guessing they'd chosen that particular morning for its proximity to May 25. Holding my sign, holding George Floyd, Breanna Taylor, and Ahmaud Arbury in the soft, pre-summer solstice light, I was unaware of that day's significance. Yet I somehow sensed that Sunday morning's synchronicity, its power. I saw the holy in those sign-bearing witnesses lining Massachusetts Avenue and heard Spirit in those affirming car horns. My inner ear heard the collective, prophetic voices, nationwide voices, urging change, urging reapportioning resources, urging affordable housing and mental health services, urging justice.

Later, when I realized that Sunday had actually been Pentecost, I did my homework. I read the Acts 2 passage describing a present-tense, filled moment that I, who also believes in a present-tense Presence, know experientially. I read the Joel 2:28 passage that Paul, biblical voice of the dispossessed and the marginalized, quotes in order to explain to the bewildered crowd why, even though they individually spoke different tongues, they could suddenly speak of "the great things God has done" as if all spoke the same language: "Therefore the day shall come," the Hebrew Bible Joel promises, "when I will pour out my spirit on all mankind; your sons and your daughters shall prophesy, your old men shall dream dreams and your young men see visions; I will pour out my spirit in those days even upon slaves and slave-girls."

And I sheepishly called my friend, Yani Burgos, who'd grown up in an evangelical family. "I have a confession to make," I told her. "Remember when you told me how important Pentecost is to you? I actually had no idea what you were talking about!" And we talked of the great things God has done.

**

"I will pour out my spirit in those days even upon slaves and slave-girls." I have a fiery reaction to that dismissive, conditional-approval-implied "even." It seems the opposite of that all-inclusive bumper sticker, "Love Your Neighbor. No Exceptions!" And reminds me of a challenging conversation I'd had with a correctional officer (CO) at a Massachusetts prison as he'd escorted me to his workplace's solitary confinement unit, the Department Disciplinary Unit. (Our prison system loves euphemisms.) On our walk from the visitors center to the DDU, past silent cell blocks and empty, weedy exercise cages, the guard quizzed me as to why I was there. And I mumbled something about being a Quaker and prison ministry.

Like most backstories, my actual response would have taken much longer than our walk: I would have had to tell that CO about my leading to find Owen and Lynda, about Owen's ministry of "trying to keep Black men out of jail," about how my Quaker meeting had gotten involved with "returning citizens," offering a weekly meal and sharing circle for ex-offenders—how I'd written to several prisoners over the years but, supported and guided by those weekly circles, had finally found the courage to actually set foot inside a Massachusetts

Correctional Institution—and therefore was there to visit one of my penpals.

Rapid-fire, stringing together keywords from Isaiah and Matthew, the CO offered me a biblical word salad: "proclaim-liberty-to-captives-and-release-to-those-in-prison-when-in-prison-you-visited-me-as-you-did-for-the-least-of-these," ending this recitation by raising his voice as if to ask a question—as if to make sure he'd gotten it right.

Startled to hear a couple of my favorite biblical passages spoken by a prison guard and, as always on these visits, struggling to stay grounded and centered, initially I'd thought he'd understood me. But later I realized his references had nothing to do with me or my prison ministry. He was telling me about his job: "Get it?" I think he'd actually meant. "Even the Bible says prisoners are a special category—they're the lowest of the low. They're the least of these. They're scum. You come here once a month. That's nice and all. But I have to deal with these people 24/7. It's my job. This is how I feed my family."

"Even upon slave girls." On a subsequent trip, a woman CO escorted me to the DDU. She'd set a brisk pace for our walk. I quickly found out why. Those tomb-like units suddenly came to life. Catcalls, hoots, insinuating comments—it seemed like every man, unseen but easily heard through the open windows, had something to say. "I know you know who this voice is," one man called. As if she had every reason to recognize his voice. As if she and he had a relationship, something special going on. As if she were his. And I realized that, just like the world outside those prison walls, an attractive woman, even one wearing the uniform of a correctional officer, can be treated like property.

How I would have loved to talk about my fiery reaction with Lynda! But Lynda died on March 20, 2018, at the age of seventy—much too soon. As her brother, Dr. Edward M. Barksdale Jr., noted at her memorial service: "Although [Reverend Cardwell and Dr. Woodruff] fought like soldiers in armed combat, their scars and wounds were internal, and many of those have affected their lives and maybe even the length of their life."

※※

June 31, 2020, the first day in Massachusetts when no new deaths from COVID-19 are reported, I step out onto my porch just as my former advisee walks past. They see me: "We both still here?" they shout. "Thank God!"

※※

Before I'd begun this apprenticeship, in moments of love or gratitude or wonder or forgiveness, in moments when wholeness and I were one and the same, I'd welled up. I still do. My tears feel different now, though, as if I'd only heard the violins before but can now hear cellos and the double basses. Welling up is richer, deeper, fuller, more nuanced. What I experience when I cry is exquisite, moving—and in a minor key. So were I to memorialize these tears into my hair-wreath in progress, I might twine and shape and twist strands of hair into the ∫ of a double bass's sound hole—or the shape of a ladle.

"Belonging confers a feeling of worth and value, which, in turn, filters into our whole being as a blessing."
Francis Weller[78]

The next Buddha will be a Sangha.

–Thich Nhat Hanh

Although there have been many restorative, contemplative times when I have been alone and filled, for much of my life I have been in community. Our peripatetic family finding itself in new surroundings again and again, our six-person unit had a strong sense of itself, honed, perhaps, by all those hours spent in cars. At a cloth napkins and fieldstone fireplace and relish-plate restaurant in upstate New York, for example, the hostess had seated us at a large, round table in the center of the dining room. I remember how our family gradually took over that public space. Delighted to order our favorites off a menu, we'd laughed, teased, repeated old stories; we quoted our favorite Stan Freberg lines.[47] We weren't loud; we weren't boisterous. But there were six of us. (The hostess began to seat diners in the corners of the room and as far away from us as possible.) Sensing watchful eyes surrounding us, we were aware of ourselves as an *us*.

In August of 1960, after a challenging first year in Lynchburg, a worse-for-wear us headed north, for Cape Cod, in our lime-green station wagon, my parents having recognized how disjointed and at-sea we were. Our us would include our grandfather that summer, so my parents rented a spacious, nineteenth-century, hip-roofed house facing Cape Cod's Bass River, with an accessible first-floor bedroom and bath for wheelchair-using Grandpa. Debby and Benjy swam at the little beach in front of the rental; Paul and I took sailing lessons at the nearby sailing school, but much of that August was spent about a mile downstream, as the seagull flies, at the Wild family compound known as "Idlewild," where we swam, sailed, and partied with multiple generations of relatives. Located near its mouth where the tidal Bass River flows into Nantucket Sound, the family compound's capacious, gambrel-roofed main house had been built by Frank Wild in 1890;[48] its broad, shady porch offered Grandpa an excellent view of the river, the granite-ribbed breakwater across the way, the sailboat-dotted Sound, and an expanded, sunburned, boisterous us.

One hot August afternoon, my second cousins otherwise occupied, fifteen-year-old me had fallen in with a group of bored, aimless teenagers whose greater Boston families summered on the Cape. Writing this, I can smell that redolent, late-summer hay smell when parched August lawns turn to straw; I smell Coppertone, too. I see the four or five of us, more girls than boys, in madras Bermuda shorts and polo shirts, our noses peeling, as we stroll along River Street, the river to our right.

"There's a trampoline in the Churchills' yard," somebody offered. So off we went. "They're Quakers," someone informed me as we walked along. Oh. (At that age, my only association with "Quaker" would have been the movie *Friendly Persuasion* and a young, memorable Anthony Perkins weeping over his rifle aimed at "Johnny Rebs.")

The Churchills lived in an actual cape: a weathered, silver-shingled, sprawling cottage. Do I remember fruit trees and a garden and a circling sprinkler? One of us went around to the screened back door—I'm seeing its wood frame painted a dark green—to ask permission to use the trampoline. A young blond person, slightly older than the rest of us, peered through the screen and then stepped outside to give our little group a quick once-over. Comfortable, apparently, she'd nodded. And said something, something gentle and trusting, before going back inside.

If I were to put what she'd told us into Quakerese, I'd say she'd appealed to that of God in us. Wordlessly, the four or five of us got that. We looked at each other; we, too, nodded. *We've been deemed trustworthy*, we realized. *Let's not mess this up.*

A word about trampolines and pre-Title IX gym class for girls: In those ancient times, women's athleticism was generally treated as an afterthought. Or a joke. Every week, several classmates claimed to have their periods and sat on the bleachers gossiping and snickering while the rest of us grimly played dodgeball. Cowering, we stood as close to the gym's back wall as possible to protect ourselves from that one mean-spirited student on the other team who always threw as hard as she could. Accurately, too. (There was always that one.) Our gym teachers drilled us on the rules of volleyball but nothing about functioning as a team. Because why would we need to know? We'd never play football under stadium lights, would we? Worse was the reduced and frustrating version of basketball we played back then, one team in pinnies, the other not, on a half court, and only allowed to dribble three times before, pivot, pivot, pivot on one planted leg, passing the ball to a teammate.

But when we used the trampoline, gym class got deadly serious. Standing around the trampoline, as close together as possible, we'd brace, hands up, ever ready to catch our jumping classmate before she cracked her head wide open or broke her neck. Or so we'd been instructed. Our whistled, sneakered gym teachers' fears surrounding us, when it was our turn in the middle, we barely bounced.

That desultory August afternoon, to be allowed to use that trampoline without adult supervision and experience unfettered joy when it was my turn seemed extraordinary. Special. Exotic. "Quakers are just different," I decided. I'd liked that difference—although I couldn't name it. And wanted more of whatever-it-was. (But how?)

"Be patterns, be examples," George Fox coached. That young Quaker at the screen door, nearly my age but who'd grown up in a very different family from mine, patterned how to acknowledge and bring forth the best in one another. I'd noted this; our Coppertone-scented group did, too. Like my gym class surrounding a trampoline with our supportive hands outstretched, we'd silently agreed to live up to what was expected of us. We'd be our best selves. Collectively.

**

Weller writes about our species' need for community—how we are born craving a village. My family sensed this, too. A unit unto ourselves, my parents nevertheless drove us to church and Sunday school every week; we'd socialized and made lifelong friends with other Unitarian Universalist families in Melrose and Stow, Massachusetts, in Syracuse and Rochester, New York—even in Bible-belt Lynchburg and Huntsville, Alabama. That our family had been part of small but vibrant communities in those latter two cities as the Civil Rights movement unfurled now seems a miracle.

One unfurling took place in Lynchburg a few months after our family returned from Cape Cod. In December of 1960, at Patterson's Drug Store on Main Street, a racially mixed group of college students staged Lynchburg's first sit-in—a few blocks from First Unitarian Church of Lynchburg,

To white Lynchburg, that historic sit-in seemed to come out of nowhere, but like the Black Lives Matter movement or the Defund the Police initiative, many meetings and much planning had gone into that early Civil Rights demonstration. While Paul and I took sailing classes—"If you can sail on Bass River, you can sail anywhere," our teacher assured us—that summer, other young people, people of color, had been trained in civil disobedience and nonviolence; they'd role-played what to do should, say, at a drug store lunch counter sit-in, an angry white person pours ketchup on your head.

I'd just turned sixteen that December; Lynchburg's first Civil Rights movement protest barely registered with self-involved, adolescent me, who knew what "port" and "starboard" meant but had never heard the words "civil disobedience." At the time, it seemed First Unitarian took no note either. Decades later, urged by Lynda to understand all I could about her and Owen's "context" for their own historic action, I'd read up on Lynchburg's Civil Rights history. At Lynchburg's Legacy Museum of African American History, a gingerbread-rich Victorian converted into well-lit, well-designed exhibition spaces, I'd listened to recordings of sit-inner Rachel Owen, a student at Randolph-Macon Woman's College in 1960, for example. She'd explained that the only "racially integrated places" in Lynchburg where those Black and white college students could safely meet, plan, and train had been Black-owned restaurants and pool halls. Hearing her weary and despondent voice, I'd been furious that my village, my faith community hadn't offered its sanctuary for those meetings. Or, on that cold December night after the sit-inners had been arrested, why hadn't members of our church stood outside the Lynchburg jail alongside other faith congregations? Why hadn't we UU members held candles and sung?

But as *Way Opens*'s subtitle reminds me, I had been on a spiritual journey; the anger, the righteous anger that arose in me as I'd sat in the museum's tiny library listening to that tape had been where I was on that path.

Where am I now? In midst of this apprenticeship, this Leading 2.0, I am moved to ask a different question: When I'd felt such anger at First Unitarian, what other feelings might that anger have masked?

And I think of learning to sail on Bass River—how Paul and I had been instructed to think layered. We'd learned to pay constant attention to wind, of course, the gusty wind off the ocean—how it differed from wind over the broad, warmer-water river. We made allowances for how the wind shifted and often died down as we sailed closer to shore. Ever mindful how that tidal river ebbed and flowed, we kept a careful lookout for hazardous sandbars at low tide. Most important, the river's surface water might appear to be moving upstream, the tide might be rising, but Bass River's deeper current inexorably moved toward the sea.

My feelings of twenty years ago had been layered. Some, like shame and chagrin, had been like sandbars. The waters recede, and there they are, undeniable and wood-against-sand grating. Guilt happens. Shame is made visible. I'd blamed my village rather than acknowledge that sandbar: my own deeply uncomfortable shame that, when Lynda and Owen first arrived at E.C. Glass, like my mother, like many white people, "I hadn't done enough." (What relief when my self-disgust, my shame re-submerged!)

And then there's the chagrin—that sinking feeling when you come up against your own stubborn refusal to acknowledge what you know—but there it is. I'd seen a shadowed, entrenched sandbar below the surface. But because Paul and I had blithely sailed over it, I pretended I hadn't seen how insidious and pervasive our nation's systemic racism is. Twenty years ago, I'd known that sandbar was there. Yet, like a petulant adolescent, I'd whined, "If well-meaning people like the Lynchburg UUs had spoken up, if they had acted back then, things would be much better now."

Would they?

Another feeling could have been *philia*—my love for my community—if I'd allowed myself to experience that love. Seemingly, my village failed to act. Yet quietly, determinedly, those good people could have responded behind the scenes— just as other white people had done throughout the South. In fact, I'd read such first-person accounts at the Legacy Museum. I'd known *tikkun olam*[49] is often not visible. Just as I'd "known" that, as another spiritual advisor, Cathy Whitmire, once said, "People are doing the best they can." (I'd immediately doubted her.)

But of course, then as now, like Bass River's deepest waters ever moving toward the seas: such deep sadness. For here we still are, still singing, "We shall overcome someday"; we're still heartbroken by that aspirational someday. Only now, twenty years after I'd done my Lynda-assigned homework, am I able to better grasp how I, my family, and Lynchburg's UU village were as bound to and as integral a part of our nation's ongoing oppression as nearly all white-occupied American villages.

I feel profound sadness. I feel the "grief that remains in our collective soul for the abuses of millions of individuals."[50]

When a member of that village, had I sensed this ongoing, collective grief? An adolescent, raised in a family unaccustomed to grief, ridiculed or hated for being a "Yankee," I had little emotional bandwidth left after perpetually feeling sorry for myself to more fully explore deeper, hidden, ancestral grief. Although once I'd caught a whiff of it, like a brief, summer breeze smelling of Coppertone, when a classmate from high school and I went swimming together at a nearby lake. Lying on our towels, we'd chatted: "So what would your life have been like back then?" I remember asking her, the *back then* understood to mean antebellum Virginia.

She looked at me as if to say, "I can't believe you don't know." (I got that incredulous look a lot in Lynchburg.) Patiently, she explained how she'd be living on a plantation, of course, and wearing a frilly, lacey, hooped dress and sipping something cool and delicious.

Somehow, I knew that wasn't true. Somehow, although I'd never heard of Karl Marx, I suspected she might be what Marxists would consider "working class." Certainly I'd observed that her neighborhood, with its modest ranches and scrawny trees, to be nothing like my own leafy, elegant neighborhood. I knew she didn't have a famous Virginian last name. So I'd intuited that just because she was white didn't automatically mean she would have been a member of the elite.

My classmate's illusion made me sad. That she hadn't acknowledged the cruel system of slavery surrounding her as she'd sipped that cool drink made me sad. But I didn't say anything. Inculcated to be a guest in Lynchburg who was to politely accept how things were done because I wasn't from there, I'd nodded. But silently wondered: Do all my classmates fantasize they'd been sipping lemonade? Do they all share this same myth? And if so, while they're all sitting on their verandas, do they also imagine they can hear screams as Simon Legree whips the field hands?

Some takeaways from that Coppertone-scented moment:
- I was not yet able to understand my own role in this tragic history.
- How delicious it had been to feel morally superior to a Southerner.
- My classmate's fantasy seemed make-believe, like a story a child might make up to deny something real and horrible and sad.

But, perhaps most important: lying on my towel, I had been trying to figure these things out alone. First Unitarian was too small to financially support a minister who, in that insular city, might have said aloud what I'd needed to hear. My Sunday school teachers hadn't urged me to read about the spiritual roots of the nonviolent movement. No one at First Unitarian mentioned the Patterson Drug Store sit-in in my presence; it was as though that historic arc-tipping-closer-toward-justice moment hadn't happened. My village could not provide what I'd needed or dimly yearned for.

Instead, my village offered other gifts.

Because it was too small to support a minister, Sunday morning services were conducted by members of the congregation or by local college professors. After a University of Virginia professor had sprinkled his sermon with wonderful excerpts and lyrical bits of poetry, on the drive home, I'd asked my parents, "Where do people get quotes?"

"They read lots of books," my parents told me. "They read and remember."

I could do that! My amazement that "reading and remembering and quoting" might be a job requirement was matched, in the sixties, by my elementary-school-aged students' amazement at an equally cushy job description. The art teacher at P.S. 120 in Brooklyn's Bushwick section, a hardscrabble, largely Puerto Rican neighborhood in those days, several of my students had submitted artworks to a citywide exhibition, and one of the talented student's work had been accepted. So I'd invited him and a few others to take the subway into Manhattan to see his work displayed. The exhibit had been mounted in the lobby of a midtown skyscraper; on our way from the nearest subway stop, we'd walked past several upscale apartment buildings.

"Who's that guy?" they'd wanted to know, passing another fancy-uniformed, whistle-bearing, white-gloved man. I'd explained a doorman's duties.

"That's a job?"

Like me, "a community of moods and selves under one name,"[51] First Unitarian Lynchburg was far more than its enriching lectures, its iced-orange cookies at coffee hour, its stone walls and green and white stained glass windows and vaulted ceiling, or its perceived silence during that fraught time. Like what happens in any close-knit village, that little

UU community, where I was a member of its Liberal Religious Youth (LRY), saw me.

Me. Messy, scattered, careless me. Left-handed, right-brained, terrible-at-math-and-science me. The me who'd felt God in the nighttime sky. And whose clear, buoyant voice could easily be heard "prais[ing] God from whom all blessing flow" every Sunday morning as Dad and I shared a crimson-covered *Hymns of the Spirit*.

Seen, accepted, supported, fifteen-year-old me volunteered to occasionally conduct E.C. Glass's morning devotionals for my Baptist and Episcopalian classmates, choosing Bible passages that spoke to me. Longing to fit in, yet my LRY identity central to who I was, I became a one-person traveling show, attending my Baptist and Episcopalian classmates' youth groups to talk about what it meant to be a Unitarian.

(I did that?)

Most mystifying to my parents—and to me, sometimes—was how, for over a year, every Friday afternoon, I took a bus across the James River to the Lynchburg Training School and Hospital in Madison Heights to spend time with two very special children. Once known as the Virginia State Colony for Epileptics and the Feebleminded, the training school, still called "The Colony" by local residents, was a sprawling campus of brick buildings housing foul-smelling, larger-than-classroom-sized wards.

Weekly I'd visit two wards: one was home for maybe fifteen young boys with serious mental impairments and one little boy I played ball with and read to, whose cognitive abilities were normal but who had been born without elbows or knees. (He could still kick and catch and throw, however.) In the other ward, its rows of hospital beds filled with silent, young, profoundly disabled epileptic women, I spent time with a teenaged girl, a hydrocephalic, whose physical challenges required institutionalization apparently, but again, whose cognitive abilities were perfectly normal. She in her wheelchair and I on a folding chair met in an empty little room off the ward—a private space but still very depressing. We chatted; I'd bring her movie magazines, fix her hair, paint her nails. "Why am I doing this?" I'd sometimes marvel on the bus ride home, happy to breathe in bus exhaust instead of The Colony's smell. My dinner waiting for me in the oven, my mother's and father's silent, baffled eyes told me: you can quit if you want. We'd understand.

But I didn't. I stuck it out until leaving Lynchburg to go to college. Why? In part, I think, because a religious community sustained me. I'd felt supported by that tiny, kind village.

I'd felt something else, too: sometimes when working with one of those children, I would suddenly experience a lift, a profound sense of rightness, a deep sense of perfect alignment with the entire universe, a fullness—as if filled by that God I'd praised every Sunday morning, a God amplified by the other voices of First Unitarian Lynchburg. At seventeen and still thinking of God as outward, celestial, a singular entity "from whom all blessings flow," I hadn't imagined that God/Spirit might be within me—inward. Nor could I have imagined that I would discover, as Hugh Barbour later put it, "God in the hard places."[52] Those sudden, random, filled moments at the training school were addictive—that I knew. And I wanted more.

Then, too, is a confused, dim memory of the training school's volunteer coordinator, a suited, older woman who'd interviewed me before I'd begun my stint. I seem to remember her to be Black; if memory serves, she would have been the first Black woman in authority I'd ever met.

That this dimly remembered woman might have held such a position in 1961 now seems extraordinary. Never quite sure what the rules were in Lynchburg, I was already on shaky (red clay) ground the first time I visited The Colony—where I was immediately and effusively greeted by several white people with Down's syndrome. (Virginia's Black, intellectually disabled patients were housed at another institution.) So I think that by the time I'd walked across the sprawling campus and was seated across from this mysterious and very important woman in my life, I probably decided that The Colony was a world unto itself—and well-named.

Pandemic-related travel concerns keeping me home, I am not able to in-person delve into sixty-year-old training school records, archived at the Library of Virginia. I am currently not able to verify this dim memory. So what follows is speculative, ruminative, and, I pray, respectful.

Whoever she'd been, that volunteer coordinator managed to convey to scattered, careless, adolescent me the full weight of what I'd agreed to do. She'd made clear how those two children would count on me. How important my weekly visits would become for them. How I mustn't let them down.

I'd heard her. Of course I couldn't quit! (When in my thirties and serving as the volunteer coordinator for the Hartford (CT) Public Schools, I would give that same lecture. Many times.)

The right-brain, intuitive, oddly wired part of me also wonders if my shadowed memory might be a signal from my soul. Because, as I was later to discover, the training center had a murky, horrific past. The Virginia Colony for Epileptics opened in 1912; its first superintendent, Dr. Albert Priddy, was a strong proponent of the eugenics movement. In 1916, at his urging, the institution was renamed The Virginia Colony for Epileptics and the Feebleminded. Between 1927 and 1956, over eight thousand people with epilepsy and those deemed feebleminded were forcibly sterilized.

Had I sensed such massive violation in those depressing ward's shadows?

Were I to depict this distant memory into my hair wreath, I'd take special care to mount my delicate, intricate creation of lamentation and grief an inch or two off its background. The shadow of that wreath would tell this story.

Another Colony memory, this one glaringly well-lit: while I can't remember the circumstances surrounding why I delivered my very first sermon in the training school's large, echoing hall to fifty or sixty residents and their minders, I vividly remember how badly it went. (Had this been an LRY activity? Possibly.) I wish I could report that, like Jesus told his hometown crowd at the very beginning of his ministry, "The Spirit of the Lord is upon me." But I can't. I was already dispirited by the time I stood at the school's podium and looked out at the men and women waiting to hear my sermon. For when we'd begun that morning's prescribed liturgy and sang our first hymn together, I realized that most worshippers couldn't read. They'd stood, randomly opened their hymnals, and holding these opened books on their outstretched hands, they'd opened their mouths wide to loudly and joyfully sing in tongues—almost like ululating. Their actual words were unintelligible. "This service isn't about words," I realized, panicked, thinking about the sermon I'd labored over—which probably contained some carefully-chosen quotes. But although I had struggled to use simple, straightforward, easily understood language, clearly I'd needed to embrace a very different modality.

"Deep in our bones lies an intuition that we arrive here carrying a bundle of gifts to offer to the community," Weller writes. "Over time, these gifts are meant to be seen, developed, and called into the village at times of need. To feel valued for the gifts with which we are born affirms our worth and dignity."[53] My shame at that misguided ministerial experience sloughed off, one Sunday morning, the same nudge that prompted me to preach at the training school or conduct morning devotionals at E.C. Glass nudged again. So during coffee hour, I'd approached one of First Unitarian's older members standing at the back of that lovely church near the refreshment table. Quiet, gentle, courtly, a doctor, as I remember, he was exactly the right man to ask the question I'd wanted to ask: "Could you accept me as your minister?"

Reader, he said yes.

I never went to divinity school. I made other choices, many unwise. But that nudge to minister, to praise God, to experience God in the hard places? It has endured.

**

It tolls for ye: one Memorial Day weekend at meeting for worship, I'd sat beside an open window, contemplating the impending holiday. (Recalling this moment, I'm tempted to add, "as all over Harvard Square, church bells rang out in honor of our nation's war dead," but I think that might just be a cinematic or Grandma add-on.) As I always did when thinking about Memorial Day, I lapsed into a well-worn thought pattern: "as long as we continue to celebrate and honor our war dead, we will continue to have war dead"—an idea passionately expressed in the 1964 movie *The Americanization of Emily*, written by Paddy Chayefsky. My favorite line, delivered by a very young, very handsome James Garner: "We perpetuate war by exalting its sacrifices."

So on that lovely, early summer Sunday morning, with or without church bells, I ritually thought these things and again remembered that movie scene. I remembered the young, curly haired James Garner. In my head, I again heard the catchy, synthesizer-played theme song to Garner's later TV series, *Rockford and Son*. As always at Memorial Day weekend's meeting for worship, I was stuck.

That morning, however, like a painter who has never before used the color red but can no longer pretend that primary hue doesn't exist, I allowed myself to go deeper. I allowed myself to mourn. Terrified to move beyond my yearly ritual yet held and loved and supported by the faith community seated all around me, my community, my Quaker village, I allowed myself to contemplate war, its cost, its losses. I allowed myself to actually feel the stories of the lichened, weathered Brookside Cemetery tombstones where, every Memorial Day when my family had lived in Stow, my Brownie troop laid crepe-paper decorated, pint-sized berry baskets filled with early summer flowers on the graves of Stow's veterans. I let myself inwardly gasp, again, at the fearsome sight of acres and acres and acres of stark, white gravestones at San Diego's Fort Rosencrans National Cemetery. I thought about mothers, centuries of mothers—about all the grieving mothers.

Could I possibly take in such enormous grief?

Overwhelmed by my brief journey into this long-dreaded realm yet aware that I was intact, whole, still in one piece, that

Sunday it came to me that to honor such enormous grief, as in to be honorable, a woman of integrity, authentic, ever-mindful, meant I was to acknowledge the impossibility to ever fully grasp this enormity. Yet to never look away.

Were I to honor this brief but unforgettable journey in my emergent hair wreath, I would shape tears, many of them. I would dot that wreath with these tears. Red tears, red hair, not as belonging to a natural-born redhead but the fire-engine red out of a box or a bottle, an artificial hue. The color of blood. The color of STOP.

**

"They're Quakers": one reason I'd been willing to tell my skeptical Glass classmates about Unitarianism had been about efficiency, I think. Whenever I met someone new in Lynchburg, the order of questions went something like this: "What's your name?" "What church do you go to?" and "Unitarian? What's that? Some kind of Yankee religion?" Raised in a *Cheaper by the Dozen* family, had I been frustrated by those inefficient, one-to-one conversations, so wanted to address more than one person at a time? (Whether one-to-one or at an Episcopal Church youth group, the outcome would be exactly the same, however. Listeners were polite and remained skeptical.)

Looking back, I think another impulse or yearning was at work: I'd longed for an immediate and, yes, efficient religious identity. At Girl Scout camp, even when we swam, the Catholic girls wore delicate gold chains around their necks strung with gold medallions of saints and a crucifix; the Jewish girls wore a Star of David necklace. I'd envied these silent statements. Catholicism did not speak to my condition but, niece of two Jewish uncles, roommate of Jewish classmates in college, enamored with a series of Jewish men, one of whom I married a month after college graduation, Judaism did. Briefly, I'd explored converting. But although its conversion ritual of the total-cleansing mikveh really appealed to swimmer-me, ultimately, I could not see myself becoming Jewish. So, for much of my early adulthood, I remained spiritually unaffiliated.

What had my soul yearned for? To be seen, known, understood within an identifiable context and, personifying that touted pattern or example, to be accountable because of that identity. I remember when this "I better be a person of integrity because I'll make all Quakers look bad if I'm not" first hit me at work. The workplace circumstances are not interesting. What interests me now is that my sense of uber-responsibility had not been about being the perpetual big sister nor was it from guilt or fear or shame. Instead, I'd experienced a clarifying, grounding, satisfying sense of alignment—there's that useful word again—with, say, those early Quakers who'd refused to barter and told potential buyers: "This is a fair price." Because it was. Dealing with Quakers saved time; Quaker trustworthiness was their brand. "Quakers did well by doing good," my efficiency-loving Dad used to say. Like nose-peeling younger me, I yearned to be my best self—with a little help from my f/Friends.

I also remember the exact moment when, in my late thirties, having decided to become a Quaker, I discovered that Quakers could be just as annoying and obnoxious and far from perfect as anyone else. That I witnessed this eye-opening moment with my first Quaker-based sangha, also known as the Ad Hoc Lunch Committee, made that *eww* moment almost palatable.

In those days, Friends Meeting at Cambridge offered two meetings for worship on Sunday mornings, each for an hour, one at 9:30 and the other at 11. Our committee, which included Ex-Husband Number 2, Chris Jorgenson, and Eric Beutner, who would later hold me as I sobbed in his arms, attended the first meeting. During the second meeting for worship, we'd talk about that morning's messages as we chopped carrots or washed lettuce for the soup, salad, bread-and-peanut-butter lunch. (We'd asked for a small donation to cover our costs; our devoted crew supplied the ingredients, the loaves of bread, and one of us made the soup ahead of time.)

The exact moment when the scales fell from my eyes? Helping to serve the soup, I spotted a middle-aged woman pick up a slice of whole-grain, organic, artisanal bread, examine it closely, bring it close to her nose to sniff it, grimace, and then put it back in the bread basket. Unable to reconcile the lofty ideals of Quakerism with such crass behavior—I would experience plenty more *eww* moments in the coming weeks and months and years—I'd walked home that afternoon with a raging headache. (Later, much later, I was able to wonder, with genuine compassion, if that woman hadn't had a complicated relationship with food. And in that bread-sniffing moment, which I'd experienced as very public, she'd thought of herself as completely alone with that challenging relationship. And struggled.)

That Sunday lunch crew (structurally, FMC's multitudinous standing committees, its ad hoc committees, its interest groups, and its working groups are a hot mess) offered me my first experience of "Quaker gossip." Yes, we'd all believed there is that of God in everyone, even in the bread-sniffing lady. Compassion, mutual support, the desire to, as Weller put it, "affirm [one another's] worth and dignity"; everyone on our crew believed in that; we tried to practice that affirmation. We could also sniff at outrageous behavior, though; we could snicker, we could still wonder aloud as we washed dishes or stored food, "Can you believe what so-and-so did or said today?"

Our sangha talked about how the spoken messages during meeting for worship resonated, too. Or hadn't. We talked about how Spirit moved through our lives. We talked about what had come up for us during silent worship. We shared our backstories—how our past experiences informed our listening.

A favorite story: as noted, everyone on the committee took responsibility for one entrée each week, but for whatever reason one Sunday—no bread. We'd pulled a frozen loaf or two out of the freezer, and Charlie Kellogg opened the oven door to shove those frozen bricks inside when, lo, there, in the oven, were several loaves of bread wrapped in aluminum foil.

We'd all inhaled. "It's a miracle!" someone whispered.

Charlie looked up and grinned. "I didn't know *he* used aluminum foil," he marveled.

We'd all heard Charlie linger over those two letters; we'd collectively chuckled. Charlie was being intentionally provocative. After all, hadn't we all pretty much agreed over slicing and dicing that Spirit was not male and might actually be more a verb than a noun?

An important bit of the "How I Became a Quaker" story that didn't make it into *Way Opens*—because I wasn't yet ready to tell it—is this: when I'd met Ex-Husband Number 2, he'd been going to Harvard Divinity School. (And the reason why the house I still live in is so close by!) That we'd both been spiritual had been central to our relationship; we'd shopped around for a greater-Boston faith community we could both love. After a couple of unsatisfactory visits, he'd said, "You know, there was this woman at school. She's a Quaker. She actually conducted a Quaker meeting with our class and—"

I'd interrupted. "I've been to a couple of Quaker meetings! I loved them. Let's try."

So the following Sunday, he and I walked to Friends Meeting at Cambridge. As we approached FMC's driveway, his divinity school classmate, Wendy Sanford, author of *These Walls Between Us: A Memoir of Friendship Across Race and Class*[54] and now one of my closest friends, spotted us and came forward to greet us. Tall, blond, utterly lovely, Wendy was not unlike the young, trampoline-owning Quaker at the Churchill's back door. I remember Wendy back-lit. I remember she'd glowed. And I was enchanted all over again.

No, Ex-Husband Number 2's and my marriage didn't last. But we have three strong and brilliant and resilient daughters together. And, like *Casablanca*'s Rick and Ilsa, "We'll always have the lunch committee!"

**

Though a Black Lives Matter sign may hang in front of the meetinghouse and a handful of people belong to this community who are not white, like First Unitarian Lynchburg, Friends Meeting at Cambridge is a white-occupied American village. And when it comes to real-life inclusivity, again and again, my spiritual home struggles—stumbles. A painful story I am compelled to tell: a few years ago, I'd attended an FMC-sponsored workshop on income disparity offered by a young member of our meeting, Ben Ehler, who, at the time, worked for United for a Fair Economy.[55] What I'd learned about the bottom-line differences between Black and white families proved a hundred-fold more dire than I'd previously understood. Unable to acknowledge my grief, guilt, shame, and anger when confronted with the harsh economic truths Ben so ably presented, I'd done what I've so often done: efficiently deny my feelings and just as efficiently move into fix-it mode—to immediately talk about reparations. Another workshop attender, a woman of color, commented, "If Quakers can't make reparations happen, what hope do we have?"

That hopeful woman no longer attends FMC. She may have moved away; she may, like other people of color, have felt unheard, unsafe, unhappy, and uncomfortable in a glaringly white space. Although more of our meeting's younger Friends have taken on leadership positions, and the outward face of FMC now has more people aged eighteen to thirty-five-ish these days, how daunting it must be for a person of color to enter a large, balconied, silent meetinghouse where a hundred or so white people, many of us white-haired, sit in silence.

And this must be said: while white Friends may take pride in Quaker's abolitionist and Underground Railroad history, in fact, like every other white-occupied village, Quakers, too, share a racist past.[56] And, as Friends of color are compelled to repeatedly point out, that hateful legacy endures, much as many white Quakers wish to deny it. Much as this faith community yearns to be loving and inclusive, much as FMC longs to put faith into action or, as Lynda would say, "get to the doing part" and, for example, join other faith communities working on reparations, we're not there. Yet.

Yes. Yet. For in spite of all our latent and overt racism and microaggressions and blunders and stumblings and cluelessnesses, deep in my heart, I do believe that hopeful woman's trust in Quakers will be realized, someday. (And, of course, wanting to bend that arc ever closer, not nearly soon enough.)

In spite of all the bread-sniffing I have observed over the years, in spite of all the ways members of my faith community remind me that we're all deeply flawed humans, I still believe that there is that of God within all of us—even within impatient, judgey, deeply flawed me. For again and again, whether at a small committee meeting or a larger gathering such as a meeting for business, when thirty or forty or fifty people gather to discern what we are collectively called to do, I have witnessed Spirit incarnate. I have seen what Love can do. I have seen how a group of our species, responsive to Spirit's prompting, can be far more wise and thoughtful and, well, better than the sum of its parts. FMC will get there. Someday.

An observation: if I have learned nothing else during the past five years, I now more fully grasp the enormity, the scale, the immense and insidious scope of this country's racism. I will say that again: if I have learned nothing else during the past five years, I now more fully grasp the enormity, the scale, the immense and insidious scope of this country's racism. Like that come-to-Jesus moment at Ben's workshop, I am humbled by this turn-an-aircraft-carrier-around-sized magnitude of what I had not understood. Truly, here, too, is God in the hard places. And I believe that my faith community, like other white-occupied villages, now shares this deeper understanding of how much we must overcome.[57]

Let us then try what Love will do. Together.

**

As with the word "apprenticeship," I have a very specific and nostalgic association with the word "village." During the turbulent summers of 1968 and 1969, my first husband and I had been staff members at Shaker Village Work Group,[58] a ten-week summer camp for adolescents located in the evergreen-rich Berkshires. Occupying the site of the former Mount Lebanon Shaker community, Shaker Village Work Group's proximity to Hancock Shaker Village, a popular tourist site just down the road, meant curious visitors traveling along Route 20 followed signs to our village, too.

To this day, if I smell a pine tree on a warm summer day, I am again twenty-four and living and working in that funky, querulous village. I'm seated outside the pine-shaded craft store next to the herb garden, a new batch of future SVWG tour guides surround me. We've just shared some peppermint tea, one of the craft store's best sellers, and reviewed how to write up a sales slip. Now comes the hard part: explaining to sixties-era teenagers that being our village's tour guide means doing your homework on Shaker history and culture—I will provide whatever resources they'll need—and being polite and accessible, too.

Like their fellow "villagers," many hailing from metropolitan New York City, those adolescent trainees ate, slept, took workshops, and replicated Shaker crafts in restored Shaker buildings. My ex-husband, for example, taught villagers how to make Shaker brooms. (While Shaker crafts, values, and work ethics were touted, much to the relief of the sexually active "villagers," Shaker Village Work Group tacitly discounted the fundamental principle of the Shakers: celibacy!) Tasked with deciding their brief-duration village's governance (both summers they'd chosen the town meeting form of direct democracy), those barefoot, long-haired teens, living on the grounds of a nineteenth-century utopian community, struggled to create their own. And just like the original inhabitants of Mount Lebanon and just like FMC, those villagers often came up short.

This gap between a *Beloved Community*[59] and what actually happens when human beings live communally was exactly what the founders of Shaker Village Work Group, Jerry and Sybil Count, had, well, counted on, I think, when they'd begun Shaker Village Work Group in 1947. What complicated, paradoxical, rich experiences those adolescent villagers had. Staff members did, too.

Having encountered this gap between the ideal and the actual many times over the ensuing fifty years, I will find myself singing the same Shaker hymn our scruffy village often sang: "More Love." Especially this bit:

> If ye love not each other
> In daily communion,
> How can ye love God,
> Whom ye have not seen?

Recently, in the midst of yet another tussle with my own faith community and again grimly humming "More Love," a story came to me: originally, two of Shaker Village's buildings had been the two halves of a chair factory. In one building, the men built wooden chairs from pine, maple, ash, birch—trees harvested from Mt. Lebanon's property. In an adjacent building, the women wove rush or cotton tape known as "listing," to cane those chairs. The story goes—if I remember correctly—that in the nineteenth century, the two buildings had been connected by a second-story, wooden walkway. When the men completed a chair, one Shaker man would walk halfway across this walkway, leave the chair, then walk back to the men's building where he would ring a bell signaling that it was safe for a Shaker woman to fetch.

It's that halfway point, isn't it, that shared, co-created place in between, that center of the room—that's where the work is. We flawed, judgey, bread-sniffing humans sit in a circle. What we collectively create, the work, is at the center. It's the work; that's what matters.

What are we called to do to help mend this world?

**

Circles happen: almost every Wednesday night for the past thirteen years, Friends Meeting at Cambridge has hosted a meal and a sharing circle for "the formerly incarcerated and those who care about them."[60] Our circle is the outgrowth of another sharing circle begun years ago in Boston's Jamaica Plain neighborhood; we have replicated the JP circle's thoughtful rituals. We, too, eat dinner together first, our shared meal in the commodious Friends Room—a gourmet meal lovingly and bounteously prepared by my husband. (Cooking is his ministry; he also helps to prepare FMC's Sunday lunch.) After cleanup, we, too, set up chairs around a cluster of flickering candles but, because our sage-cleansing ceremony has set off FMC's smoke detectors once too often, summoning an embarrassing convoy of Cambridge Fire Department equipment to Longfellow Park, rain or shine or freezing temperatures, we troupe outside to ritually cleanse ourselves. The lights turned off in the Friends Room, we sit in a circle around the flickering candles. We review the circle's guidelines and values. An ornately carved walking stick is passed clockwise; only the person holding this talking piece may speak. Like the JP circle, our time together ends with the Serenity Prayer.

These days, Zoom offers another, pared down, and far-less-satisfying version: no meal, no sage, no physical circle, no candles, no talking piece, no closeness or breathing in harmony with one another, and when we say the Serenity Prayer together? It's pretty raggedy. Sadly, several members of our circle have decided not to do Zoom and have opted out.

Like so many mixed outcomes because of this pandemic, not being able to perform the sage ceremony has been both a loss and an unplanned and welcomed opportunity to reflect on this sometimes-questioned ritual. Over the years, some circle attenders have rightly pointed out that this practice comes from a Native tradition—and is therefore an appropriation. I respect that. Other circle members do, too. When we can all safely meet again in person, however, I will share a recent opening.

The backstory to this opening: inspired by a wonderful poem by Judith Offer, "On Studying Sacred Texts" [Appendix B], during Covid Summer 2020 at our pre-meeting for worship forums, various members of the FMC community took turns reflecting on various writings, like Martin Luther King Jr.'s "Letter from Birmingham Jail" or Arundhati Roy's "The Pandemic Is a Portal."

Technically, one sacred text we twenty-first century Quakers studied that summer, "Skywoman Falling," isn't a text; it comes from the oral tradition. Although this printed creation story from the Shenandoah and George people begins Robin Wall Kimmerer's seminal book, *Braiding Sweetgrass,* for generations, "Skywoman Falling" has been told as people sat around a fire. A little like a sharing circle?

Had the JP sharing circle originator, Father Brian Murdock, understood humans' shared circle history? Had he and others intuitively replicated rituals our ancestors had performed? Had he remembered that all humans once sat around fires?

When members of our Prison Fellowship Committee first visited the JP circle, we were told that, because prison lighting had been so harsh and obtrusive, returning citizens would relish a sharing circle's dim, gentle, soothing lighting. Yet don't all of us, returning citizens or not, prompted by the lingering smell of burning sage and the flickering candles in the middle of a circle, remember from the deepest part of ourselves when we'd sat around a fire and told the stories of our village or had shared our own truths?

Given how dangerous making eye contact had been behind bars, the JP organizers had explained that each person seated around the circle ritualistically making eye contact before speaking to be a necessary trust-building exercise. Yet when we deeply look into another eyes aren't we, in fact, reinforcing what a nomadic community or a village does? We see each another. We value, we honor each person. We acknowledge our shared space. Like the signs in my neighbors' windows these days, we're affirming, "We're all in this together."

At that forum, after hearing how the "Skywoman Falling" story resonated with our forum speaker, I was moved to ask that "circle" of forty or fifty Zoom tiles, "Who are you in this story?" And, like our speaker, Nancy Hewitt, several people shared wonderfully open and honest answers. My answer would have been, "I am the old woman, the crone, seated near the fire to warm my old bones. I am the one telling this story. Again. Like my grandmother, I embellish here and there, add a little something someone in the circle may need to hear that night. My voice rises and falls, but when I talk about Muskrat, it becomes husky with love and gratitude."

Circles indeed happen: recently, Marty Grundy invited me to join six other Quaker women from all over the country to discuss Weller's *Wild Edge of Sorrow* via Zoom. My sense is that not one of us knew everyone before we began to meet; I'd only known Marty.

Such a brave undertaking. To discuss grief and loss—to tell painful stories from our childhoods with complete strangers? But all of us had been willing to be as open and as straightforward as the men and women of the Wednesday night sharing circle. And as happens sometimes during meeting for worship, we'd collectively become silent as we took in what had just been shared. Unable to sense the in-real-life vibe as our guided conversation ebbed and flowed, we nevertheless began to breathe in harmony. We jelled. We created a Zoom circle.

No surprise, then, that this shadowed and embellished and ornate hair wreath is of so simple yet sacred a shape—and, as noted before, misshapen—imperfect.

"We are hard-wired for ritual." Francis Weller[79]

Baked Right In

I'd like to believe that, back in the fifties, when my mother noticed a recipe for Christmas stollen in a *Ladies' Home Journal* or *Good Housekeeping*, she'd remembered eating a delicious, buttery slice of this sweet bread as a child. Charmed and warmed by this rare, vivid, happy childhood memory and wanting to share such deliciousness with her family, Mom immediately tore that recipe out.

Like for many mothers, the role of High Priestess of Good Cheer and Making Sure Everyone Has a Spectacular Christmas had been foisted upon Mom, a stressful and exhausting role made more challenging by her decidedly non-spectacular childhood holidays. And that with every move, our family's traditions and rituals became more and more indispensible. If the six of us sat down for dinner at precisely six, if, like other New England-based families, we ate salmon and peas on the Fourth of July, if we had stollen for breakfast at Christmas, if we performed the same ceremonies and rituals in Lynchburg or Huntsville we'd performed in Fayetteville or Stow, would we feel less confused, uncertain, afraid?

His own childhood Christmases decidedly merry and bright, Dad pretty much dictated our Christmas shoulds; his specifications included how tinsel should be hung—one-third of each silvery strand on the back side of each piney branch, two-thirds on the front—and how the High Priestess of Good Cheer should behave: "Not in the Christmas spirit, Pat," my holly jolly father scolded her in the weeks leading up to Christmas should my harried mother fuss, complain, nag, lose her temper. Running on empty, unable to cheerily fulfill her role, by tearing out that stollen recipe and baking that sweet bread every year, my ever-resilient mother claimed her own agency, her own inviolate and loving contribution to our Christmas rituals. Or so I'd like to believe.

But, oh dear! Many Christmases later, when my aged parents had been unable to join my husband, daughters, and me for Christmas in Somerville, my mother thoughtfully ordered us a stollen from a Harvard Square bakery. And lo, we discovered there's *wunderbar,* expertly made-in-Germany-for-centuries stollen, lightly dusted with powdered sugar and filled with orange peel, raisins, and chopped almonds—and then there's the god-awful recipe Mom had torn out! "I don't even know why I bother," she'd muttered to herself a couple years before she died, standing at my kitchen stove stirring a buttercream frosting which, traditionally served still hot, she slathered on either an under-baked or singed-at-the-edges loaf filled with disgusting, artificially colored, red and green candied fruit. "Nobody even likes stollen."

Like a remembered slice, *wunderbar* or my mother's, so much is baked into this story. So much is here, some of it imagined, some of it warm and delicious, some of it inedible and uneaten and to be pushed to the edge of an only-used-at-Christmas plate. There's the touching possibility that my mother's remembered, madeleine-like slice of stollen had been baked by one of her German relatives from her father's side of the family and savored as a toddler—before Munro abandoned his wife and two small daughters. There's the yawning, lamentable gap between my mother's love-dusted intention and the hot mess our family actually ate on Christmas morning. There's Ben, Tina, Allison, and me, all of us now eating gluten-free, understanding why our Christmas memories feel a little queasy.

But mostly there's this: like a generous roll of marzipan sometimes placed down the middle of two-halves of stollen dough and then snugly tucked inside the folded halves, at her core, my mother had been a first-rate high priestess! Within her lay reverence, awe, a deep awareness of light, mystery, wonder—and a baked-right-in instinct to solemnize her deep awareness.

Tragically, her five-person congregation never recognized Mom's ministry. Every year on the winter solstice, when she'd excitedly announce, "The days are getting longer!" we'd shrugged our shoulders. Distracted and besotted by Christmas, in the truest sense of the word, accustomed to this Christian-rooted holiday, we didn't understand.

I didn't understand. As a smart-ass young adult, if I gave any notice to my mother's yearly pronouncement or how, after she and Dad moved to Cape Cod, she'd begun to glory in the "quality of the light," I'd probably dismissed her excitement as something to do with her seasonal affective disorder—a condition she'd begun talking about. But after I began to explore my mother's "like something out of Dickens" childhood with a series of therapists, after our mother-daughter relationship deepened, after my own relationship with Light, mystery, and wonder deepened, I, too began to notice. I began to see our light-imbued world through my mother's reverent eyes. Where we differed, my efficiently rose-smelling mother and I, was about the length of those quality-of-the light-affirming moments.

Serendipitously, my light-awed mother died at age ninety-five in October of 2018, that wondrous time of year in New England when the autumn sun is low in the sky, and the world glows. One glowing afternoon, a week or so after she'd died, I'd walked past a crimson and auburn-leafed sugar maple. Prompted by its flamboyance, I opened myself up to Mom. "What do you want to teach me?" I asked out loud.

"Be grateful," came an answer. Which I heard as, "Look at the precious world around you. See it. All of it. Pay attention. Take in its beauty, its brokenness, its underdone and singed bits; be grateful you're alive to experience all of it."

Sometimes, now, I think about my mother's mother's mother and back and back and back for generations. Sometimes I let my imagination take me to a bleak, pre-Christian, midwinter's night, a fierce snowstorm raging outside, and my ancestral, multiple-great grandmother seated by a robust fire telling stories of promise and hope and the return of the light to her grandchildren. Her stories assure her confused, uncertain, afraid listeners that, yes, as the Gospel of John puts it, "The light shines in the darkness, and the darkness has never overcome it." She tells the same wondrous stories her grandmother told her but embellished and improved, of course. And like those ancestral women, like me, my harried and often-overwhelmed mother, through her ritual of keeping track of our tilted planet's journey around the sun, found sustenance, found hope, found grounding. She'd acknowledged Mother Earth beneath her feet—and where Planet A was on its journey around the sun. Briskly, no doubt! Or so I'd like to believe.

To honor my mother, to honor my ancestors, and to ground myself, every morning, a still-full mug of French roast coffee close at hand and waiting, I sleepily practice a daily ritual: like I'd already done for decades, I note that day's date and weather. But since my mother's death, I also record the time the sun will set that day, too.

Some mornings, my left hand merely propels my pen across my journal page. And some mornings, I am gifted. Those penned squiggles and jots become All, Wholeness, Awe. A date, a time—those few noted digits remind me that, a resident on this precious "pale blue dot," I am a part of an ebbing and flowing story. On consecutive bleak midwinter mornings when I note 4:15—4:14—4:13—I remind myself, "The light shines on."

And I am grateful to be reassured.

Grief work is not passive: it implies an ongoing practice of deepening, attending, and listening. It is an act of devotion, rooted in love and compassion. Weller[80]

Deepening, Attending, Listening

The American Sign Language sign for the letter "i" is to close all your fingers into a fist except your pinky, which is extended upward; to sign "I" as in oneself, you place your fist with extended pinky onto your breastbone, pinky outward, your thumb closest to your chest. The sign for "I'm talking to myself" is to make the "I" sign with both fists, rotating your closed hands so that your two pinkies meet—and to gently tap your pinkies together a few times.

When teaching deaf teenagers at a residential school, that last sign came in handy. Because sometimes, when all my student's faces became blank, I would imagine that they'd left their physical bodies and were presently cavorting together. Somewhere. In a sunny meadow, perhaps. With butterflies and buttercups and lush grass. My students just knew how to do this, I'd half-believed. (This half-fantasy had been way more a *Wind in the Willows* scenario than based on where actual twentieth-century American teenagers might hang out.) But wherever they had been, when I'd sign, "I'm talking to myself," they'd come back. They'd reenter their physical bodies. And laugh. Sheepishly. As if caught.

Sometimes, I've wondered if this leading means I'm being asked to simply talk to myself. That I am being nudged to begin this apprenticeship—to write out these stories, delve and ponder, to have long and revealing conversations with my brothers and sister about our family because of personal need. Because it is now time to begin this ongoing practice. For myself.

But as my grandma used to say, *sotto voce*, whenever out in the world and someone minimized her or talked down to her or shouted at her as if she were deaf, "Pardon my dust!" She'd meant the exact opposite. (Sarcasm is confusing for children.) Unwilling to make a scene, my venerable grandmother nonetheless claimed her dignity, her worth. At least to the adoring granddaughter within earshot.

Like Grandma, I claim my venerability. I claim "the ripeness of my cronehood." But at this portal-time when, rightfully, it is the voices of Black, Indigenous, and people of color (and, of course, our young people) we need to listen to, how grateful I am for two BIPOC women, Junauda Petrus-Nasah and Robin Wall Kimmerer, for their abiding wisdom and guidance as this apprenticeship continues.

That ripeness quote is from Petrus-Nasah's amazing poem, "Could We Please Give the Police Departments to the Grandmothers?" Writing when the police officer who'd killed Michael Brown had not been indicted, Petrus-Nasah chose to share her open-hearted vision of a healing and transformative world after George Floyd had been murdered.[61]

Junauda Petrus-Nasah's dreadlock-crowned grandmothers, who cruise the streets dispensing love and delicious food, don't look like Grandma or me. Her imagined grandmothers know oppression and white supremacy; Grandma and I know privilege. That the venerable women Petrus-Nasah describes lived profoundly different lives from the women in my family cannot and should not be discounted.

Yet, although the poet's fleet of grandmothers cruise in "bad-ass" Cadillacs, my grandma chugged along in her stately Chrysler, and I drive a no-nonsense Subaru, we can check off the same fundamental boxes: we grandmothers know our own worth. We fiercely love our grandchildren and want their lives to be sweeter. Our journeys around the sun numbered, we feel some urgency to pass on what we've seen and what we've come to understand about what matters.

**

At the end of *Braiding Sweetgrass,* Robin Wall Kimmerer writes of the desecration of Onondaga Lake and how this *Haudenosaunee* (People of the Longhouse) holy site became a Superfund site. Nine Superfunds, actually! For decades a dumping ground for industrial waste and sewage, its water supply, the crystal-clear Onondaga Creek now "run[ning] as brown as chocolate milk,"[62] once upon a time Onondaga Lake had been pristine, fish-rich, life-giving. It was here, on its shore and in the shade of a towering white pine, sometime between 1450 and 1660, that the five, warring Haudenosaunee tribes agreed to live in peace with one another and with the natural world. This agreement, known as the Great Law of Peace, created the Haudenossaunee Confederacy, a viable democracy predating the United States of America by centuries.

As Annie would advise right now: "Breathe!" For here it is, again, our devastating history. This particular story, comparable to Philadelphia's Independence Hall being bulldozed to make way for a superhighway or a parking lot, seems purposely cruel. Egregious. And as has happened from sea to shining sea, it has resulted in "generations of grief, generations of loss," Kimmerer notes.[63] (And as I read her words, I hear the tears in her voice.)

A botanist and a member of the Potawatomi Nation, when Kimmerer visits this hellish, central New York territory, her practiced eye sees what you and I might not notice. She recognizes growing things that are actually mitigating the devastation. "Plants are the first restoration ecologists," she writes. "They are using their gifts for healing the land, showing us the way."[64] How she details this ongoing restoration process, Kimmerer's deep and respectful knowledge of an emergent, spreading, interconnected ecological community, how birds and ants and fruit-bearing bushes are reciprocally working together to heal this sacred place is my favorite passage in her wonderful book.

Why? For starters, because as a mid-fifties resident of Onondaga County and a frequent traveler on the New York Thruway, I have odiferous memories of Onondaga Lake. On our numerous road trips, my family would first spot Dad's workplace, General Electric's massive Electronics Park from the highway and then, almost immediately, drive by that still, lifeless—and putrid—lake. That lake smelled so awful we'd crank up our car windows as we drove past. On one such trip, when ten or eleven, I'd noticed a couple of picnic tables situated between that foul lake and the busy, noisy Thruway. And asked my parents, "Why would anyone want to have a picnic there?" And was told, "Because some people have no other choice." On our way to ski or to summer camp or a cloth-napkins restaurant, I'd tried to imagine what such a singular, grim choice must be like. And failed.

When told matter-of-factly that unnamed people dumped chemicals into the lake and that's why it smelled so bad, do I also remember the briefest of tugs, a vague, disquieted moment of "Why is this okay?" I'd like to think I did. An avid swimmer, at that age I would have already swum in a number of upstate New York lakes—clear, lovely, Indigenous-named lakes like Seneca and Skaneateles—and, yes, I'd swum in Lake George and Cazenovia Lake, too. I have always loved fresh water; I am happiest when immersed in a no-salt, no-sharks lake or pond. A part of me I am only now beginning to recognize, a part deep in my soul, ached because of what had happened to Onondaga Lake.

Like my Lynchburg social studies teacher skipping over slavery and Jim Crow and the horrific history of the word "lynch," my Fayetteville-Manlius social studies teachers had acknowledged the Iroquois Confederacy—but skipped over where that momentous historic arc tipping closer toward justice event took place. Almost as if it hadn't happened. Or as if that lake no longer existed. Almost as if, for our teachers to have named the corporate contributors to Onondaga Lake's lifelessness, they'd known it would have meant listing the corporations their students' parents worked for: The Solvay Process Company. Carrier. And, yes, General Electric.

Helpless to stop these corporations—and other desecrators—from dumping toxic waste into their own Independence Hall, the Onondaga Nation continues to honor the covenant their ancestors agreed to centuries ago. "[T]hey have never surrendered their caregiving responsibilities. They have continued the ceremonies that honor the land and their connection to it. The Onondaga people still live by the precepts of the Great Law and still believe that, in return for the gifts of

Mother Earth, human people have responsibility for caring for the nonhuman people, for stewardship of the land."[65]

Were the Onondaga Nation's Wholeness-evoking prayers, the Nation's grief, its ceremonies, its collective, enduring love for Mother Earth what I'd sensed when walking through the woods—their woods—near my house and felt Something. Like entering a Quaker meetinghouse and knowing that the space I've just entered to be held in deep prayer by that meeting's elders, did I intuit that I'd walked on wept-over land—tears shed by living, breathing, present-day people?

Perhaps—and, yes, admittedly a stretch. How grateful I am to Robin Wall Kimmerer who prompts me to ask such a question. As I continue to learn the history I was never taught, may I continue to reexamine and perhaps retell my own history in order to make space for deeper and, possibly, more soul-imbued, mystical questions. For as this lifelong apprenticeship continues, there will always be more to ask, learn, discover.

How grateful I am, too, for what those botanical signs of restoration teach me: "A few brave trees have been established, mostly cottonwoods and aspens that can tolerate the soil. There are clumps of shrubs, some patches of asters and goldenrod, but mostly a thin scraggly collection of common roadside weeds. Dandelions, ragweed, chicory, and Queen Anne's lace blown to this spot have made a go of it. Nitrogen-fixing legumes in abundance, and clovers of all kinds, have come to do their work. That struggling field of green is, to me, a form of peacemaking," Kimmerer writes.[66]

So many take-aways here. One seems to be about radical acceptance. "That struggling field of green," filled with chicory and Queen Anne's lace and dandelions, isn't pastoral or paradisiacal and about as far from the green, storied Turtle

Island as anyone could imagine. (Although I do have a special place in my heart for upstate New York's roadside weeds.) Miraculously able to grow in toxic soil—let's remember that precious clump of mud in Muskrat's paw—these post-apocalyptical weeds are showing up.

May I learn to accept that, like those weeds "[making] a go of it" on a Superfund site, I inhabit a radically altered Earth.

Doesn't this Kimmerer passage ask us to celebrate what we might dismiss as weeds? Isn't she suggesting we reexamine our criteria for what counts, what matters? Who matters? Aren't we being asked to acknowledge the cast-offs, the ignored, the ones silently standing on the edge? Aren't we being reminded that wind, ants, seed-pooping birds are allies in this desperately needed healing work? Isn't she urging us to listen to the deep, abiding wisdom of Mother Earth herself? Aren't we being asked to regard all of these relations with love and with gratitude?

May I be more mindful of weeds.

Of all the weeds Kimmerer lists, because of its extraordinary bright blue color, chicory has always been my favorite. Sometimes called cornflower—cornflower is actually a blue descriptive—chicory and Queen Anne's lace and birdsfoot trefoil abundantly grew beside the semi-paved road leading to Big Pink. I have recently discovered that this beloved blue, associated with an early nineteenth-century period of German romanticism, "stands for desire, love, and the metaphysical striving for the infinite and unreachable."[67] How perfect.

As Kimmerer walks over that ravaged land noting unexpected signs of hope, she smells "a fragrance that haunts my memory—but then it is gone." But then, ah, later, there she is, "smiling up at me like a long lost friend." Sweetgrass.

"Tentatively sending out rhizomes through the sludge, slender tillers marching bravely away, sweetgrass is a teacher of healing, a symbol of kindness and compassion."[68]

May I always remember, "Love is the first motion."[69]

**

As if to assure me that this leading mattered and that I'm not just talking to myself but also to other white people, in August 2020, I experienced a great opening: as my meeting continued to study sacred texts at our pre-worship forums, one Sunday, guided by our presenter, Joe Tierney, we'd looked at Dr. Martin Luther King Jr.'s "Letter from Birmingham Jail."

Over the years, I have read and reread King's foundational letter on "constructive, nonviolent tension"; in preparation for the upcoming forum, I'd dutifully read it again. But that August morning, something came alive for me when I heard Joe, clearly outraged so little has changed in this country since King wrote his seven-thousand-word letter almost sixty years ago, read aloud: "One day the South will recognize its real heroes. They will be the James Merediths, with the noble sense of purpose that enables them to face jeering and hostile mobs, and with the agonizing loneliness that characterizes the life of the pioneer."

I don't know why that particular passage spoke so powerfully to Joe, but hearing him say "agonizing loneliness" opened up such grief, unexpected and overpowering.

My God! I thought, stunned. *Lynda!*

Too upset to attend meeting for worship, I clicked off Zoom—but the weight of everything Lynda had endured, her agonizing loneliness—how she'd died too soon because she'd borne our nation's cruel, ghastly history on her young shoulders and for the rest of her life—Grand Canyon-sized grief weighted me in my chair. Unable to move, I cried.

This is why I began this apprenticeship, I thought later, on a tearful, masked walk. This is what this leading has been all about. To feel and to acknowledge such cumulative pain as fully and as wholly as I can. Because, by doing so, I honor Lynda.

I'd thought Dr. Lynda Darnell Woodruff's death meant the end of being taught by her. But as my parents' deaths are teaching me and my apprenticeship reinforces, grief offers great openings. As Annie points out, we can always go deeper. "Just as going out into space in an infinite journey, so is traveling inward," Annie likes to remind us. "Inhabit your body; inhabit that inner space," she counsels. Like a slender flashlight beam or the flickering light of a single candle, an insight illuminates an inner truth; it can also shine a light on other insights, other truths waiting in that cavernous, mysterious, endless realm. There will always be more to grok. "Live up to the light that thou hast and more will be granted thee," Caroline Fox, a Quaker intellectual, promised in 1841.

And, yes, praise Spirit, on that tearful Sunday morning walk, something deep within me aligned, and more Light had been granted: "I am not alone," I realized. Others like me have felt and acknowledged this cumulative pain; other people have experienced this titanic grief. Like my masking sadness with anger, other white people have perfected their own avoidance strategies. They've looked away. They've rationalized. They've blamed, numbed themselves, denied.

Deep inside, white people know the truth. Like a global pandemic asks us, like our daily witnessing of climate change's ravages asks us, we are being asked to not look away or pretend or ignore these realities. White people cannot, presto chango, undo this shameful history nor ignore how that history still plays out. We cannot undo Earth's damage. We cannot bring back to life the millions of people who will die from this pandemic. We can't fix these outcomes, we cannot rewrite these facts. We must feel them.

To join with other voices to say this? Name this? Acknowledge this? Write this? I wondered as I walked. Is this what I am being called to do?

Yes.

Silently affirming this existential moment stirred up a memory: on my very first day at E.C. Glass, about to begin my sophomore year, a pretty, slender, brown-eyed classmate confronted me during homeroom. "You're a Yankee, aren't you?" Startled, I'd nodded. "I hate Yankees," she spit out. And then gave a brief but detailed history lesson on General William Tecumsah Sherman's march from Atlanta to the sea during the Civil War; angrily, she'd enumerated how many acres Sherman had burned, the swath of destruction he'd wreaked.

Something very powerful, something that had nothing to do with me had compelled her to leave her own homeroom that first day of school—to walk through that sprawling high school's hallways to seek me out in order to say what she'd been burning to say. To a Yankee. Any Yankee would do. I see that, now.

And I now wonder what would have happened if, instead of stammering, "That was years ago, why are you blaming me?" I'd instead met her in that place of anguish? What would have happened if I'd said something like, "What a terrible story! I can understand why you are so upset. And there are so many terrible stories, aren't there? Enslavement, lynchings, our treatment of Native peoples, the land, religious persecutions, needless, endless wars—so many! You and I share our nation's shameful history."

How should I memorialize this great opening on my wreath? With Lynda's initials made from entwined black and white strands? Do I create an infinity sign from braided hair? Or do I leave a yawning gap at the top of this wreath, at twelve o' clock, at midnight, at that existential time of reckoning—a purposed opening, an unmasking that reveals the wreath's bared, rusty, wire frame and invites whoever views this nakedness to fill in that pregnant emptiness for themselves. To ponder.

**

Soon after George Floyd's murder, Zenaida Peterson, a young person of color whose pronouns are they and them, exhausted from many sleepless nights as intrusive, TV-station helicopters filmed Black Live Matter protests in their Dorchester neighborhood, sobbed at a meeting for worship, "This is devastating! Our history is devastating!" they'd cried. And then asked: "Have you made any space to grieve?"

Many of us who attend Friends Meeting at Cambridge do not live in neighborhoods where Black Lives Matter protests happen. Many of us at that meeting for worship had not been kept awake the night before by circling helicopters. Nevertheless, holding our collective, Zoom-muted breath, we'd held Zenaida. We'd held their grief.

Their anguished query recalled this Weller passage: "Nonredemptive mourning acknowledges that some losses should never be allowed to settle, like silt, to the bottom of our memory. Some losses, such as cultures that have been forever silenced, species that have disappeared, and traumatic events that affect whole communities and cultures, should be kept present in our communal memory."[70] And so, at a called meeting for mourning held soon after Zenaida's wrenching query, I'd read that passage aloud to my meeting.

But even before Zenaida reminded us of this powerful, shared need for non-redemptive mourning, Friends Meeting at Cambridge's LGBQT+ Concern Group had created a yearly, communal space in which to grieve. Each year, on a designated Sunday afternoon, in honor of the International Transgender Day of Remembrance, November 20, our meeting remembers those transgender people, many of them women of color, who were murdered the previous year. One by one, we light a tea candle from a central, large candle; each of us picks up a three-by-five card to read aloud the memorialized person's name and brief—painfully brief—biography.

Like Annie inviting our yoga class to mentally place a chosen thing on an altar or shrine, like the copy of *Daddy-Long-Legs* beside me as I write this, like my daily recording of the time the sun will set, those soothing candles and poignant, tragically brief biographies allowed great openings. Pre-apprenticeship, pre-language to understand what I felt, in the presence of my faith community, I'd experienced another momentary but powerful—and shared—acknowledgment of the world's sorrow. For Weller also notes: "Grief has never been private; it has always been communal."[71]

Those sentimental Victorians understood this, didn't they? They'd picnicked in cemeteries; on commemorative occasions, large family gatherings were held on the family plot. Grieving middle-class and upper-class women wore color-coded clothing so as to instantly communicate their stage of mourning:

black told of recent, acute, still-raw grief. Lavender or gray clothing meant that time had passed. Letters being a major form of communication in the nineteenth century, a black-edged envelope warned the recipient to prepare themselves for dire news. Civil War casualties, high infant mortality rates, slipshod sanitation, fast-moving epidemics—the Victorians received so much terrible news through the mail.

Much Victoriana, like the bustle and the whalebone corset, has rightfully been abandoned. But as this pandemic continues, we might reconsider the Victorian purposely public acknowledgments of grief and loss. Their ability to instantly communicate to the strangers around them, as Rilke's poem perfectly puts it, "Right there I'm sort of glued together—" perhaps deserves a second look.[72]

I experienced shared, respectful, tender grief with strangers right after September 11 and then, again, in 2013, after the Boston Marathon bombing. About a week after the Twin Towers fell, my husband and I got in our car and just drove, just "got out of Dodge," eventually finding ourselves on the North Shore's Cape Ann and strolling down Rockport's Bearskin Neck. It was early evening; most of the Neck's shops and restaurants and ice cream parlors were closed. But past the commercial section, at the end of the neck, we discovered a small, circled, open space—a commemorative space perhaps, with a couple of granite benches and a long granite jetty extending beyond that circle and into the harbor. A small crowd had gathered on the jetty; they'd sat quietly on the rocks. So we joined them. Do I remember Boston's skyline faintly visible in the distance to our south? Perhaps. I certainly remember how hushed that crowd had been—how grateful I had been to be with other people, quiet, somber people, after a week of being terrified to step outside. It was almost as though they, too, had randomly driven here so that we could all be together. And to silently grieve. (I was later to learn from Lynda and Owen that many people of color did not share the horror and grief palpable in that largely white jetty crowd. Given our nation's history of lynchings, racist attacks, police brutality, and the daily macro and microaggressions they have experienced, I understand why.)

Breathe.

Like most greater Boston residents, soon after the Boston Marathon bombing of April 15, 2013, I quickly discovered how many people I knew were somehow connected to its victims or to the two Cambridge brothers who'd constructed those horrific, pressure-cooker bombs. (Three people were killed, and hundreds more lost limbs or were maimed.) Tamerian and Dzokhan Tsarnaev had lived just across the city line between Somerville and Cambridge; they'd gone to the same high school two of my daughters and many of my friends' children attended. Many people I knew had stories; many stories featured the younger brother, Dzhokhar—or "Jahar" as he had come to be called. "He was such a goofy, sweet guy!" classmates and former teachers exclaimed with genuine bewilderment. "How could this happen?" Another pressing question hung in the air: "How did affluent, progressive Somerbridge let this happen?"

My friends wondered. My yoga class wondered. My Quaker meeting wondered. And I'd like to believe that sometimes, as we'd earnestly probed, although not named, we'd collectively caught glimpses of a cavernous archive of painful, searing history—ancestral grief, as Weller calls it. "Ancestral grief also speaks to the grief that remains in our collective soul for the abuse of millions of individuals."[73]

Naming this in-our-bones grief does not in any way condone the Boston Marathon bombing. It does not condone what the Tsarnaev brothers did. It merely invites me/us to acknowledge those two young men's backstory—a tragically classic story of radicalization in times of war and upheaval.

Breathe.

My second community-shared grief story—which may not be factual—happened on the T's Red Line a couple of weeks after the bombing. At the Charles Street/MGH Station, a young, lean, drawn-faced woman got on and sat maybe five feet away. She began to sob. Uncontrollably. I handed her a mauve, flowered handkerchief that she quickly saturated. And like that hushed, shared moment with those seated on the Rockport jetty, the others on that mostly empty subway car just breathed. We breathed together.

No one on that train knew if that sobbing woman was a runner or if she'd just visited a fellow runner, of course—although she'd looked like one. And the Red Line T stop "MGH" means Massachusetts General Hospital—where over thirty bombing victims, some of whom had just crossed the finish line when the nail-filled bombs exploded, had been rushed. But like the elders at a Quaker meeting who silently hold the space for Spirit, we strangers held that space for her. Because each of us, in ways we had no way to understand, somehow connected with her anguish.

**

A couple of days after the world learned that Donald Trump was to become the next president of the United States, FMC offered a called meeting for worship. Still stunned by this unexpected news, grateful to sit with others, and riven by fear and anger, finding that inner peace that passeth understanding seemed pretty much impossible.

Something came to me: "Be sand in the machine."

Immediately I signed up for civil disobedience training to be offered at nearby Cambridge Friends School. "What's to learn?" an aging activist wondered when I told him what I'd planned to do. "Ya go limp. Period."

But after seventeen years of working with adult learners, I know my own learning style: I need experienced teachers—and who better than two women from ACT UP—veterans of the AIDS-pandemic actions of the eighties. I need to pay. I need an all-day workshop with role-playing, break-out groups, good conversations over a brown-bag lunch. I need hand-outs.

More importantly, to listen to those ACT UP trainers' stories, to role-play and to break bread with others at that workshop, some of whom I already knew, elucidated an important realization: I am only one grain. And why I feel so helpless and lonely and afraid sometimes. I need to grate in community. Sensing that connecting with other churches and synagogues and mosques might be a critical first step, I'd asked Friends Meeting at Cambridge if I could represent FMC at the monthly gatherings of Cambridge faith communities convened by Cambridge's Mayor Denise Simmons. My request was approved.

At one such meeting, held in the mayor's elegant Cambridge City Hall, Rahsaan Hall, Director of the Racial Justice Program of the ACLU, spoke. "Share your values," he'd begged the gathered group. "People are confused right now. They're looking for a moral compass."

Many who'd heard Hall's plea that morning would eventually form the Cambridge Interfaith Sanctuary Coalition (CISC) in March of 2017. Comprised of eleven Cambridge faith communities, FMC among them, CISC very publicly offered a young, undocumented Ecuadorian mother and her two small daughters sanctuary in University Lutheran Church ("UniLu"), in the heart of Harvard Square. (The family's living space and a room for volunteers had been created from what had been UniLu's Sunday school classrooms and offices.)

Why do I note "very publicly"? Because one of the basic tenets of the Sanctuary Movement is exactly what Hall had been talking about: for people of faith to collectively declare this is our testimony to the whole world.[74] Through local and national news outlets, CISC emphatically publicized that this undocumented mother and her children were being housed and fed and the children accompanied to parks and playgrounds by United Church of Christ members, Jews, UUs, Harvard Divinity School students, Baptists, Quakers, Lutherans, Episcopalians, and others.

Because Immigration and Customs Enforcement (ICE) might pound on UniLu's door at any time, CISC organized around-the-clock volunteer presence. Some three hundred fifty volunteers, having received training should ICE agents show up, then signed on for paired, four-hour shifts. (The designated volunteers room had been equipped with Wi-Fi, comfortable chairs, reading lamps, a bulletin board giving the latest ICE updates, and two twin beds.) Twenty-five or so volunteers from Friends Meeting at Cambridge, my husband and I among them, participated.

Over time, this enormous accompaniment effort felt less and less like what I felt called to do and those weekly meetings at Somerville City Hall more what Spirit asked of me. But to have been a part of this aligned, sand-in-the-machine initiative for a couple of years—to have had brief yet warm, energizing conversations with other allies before and after each shift had been balm.

And now I see that each heart-pounding shift would prove a series of four-hour dress rehearsals for this ever-anxious, ever-fearful, protocols-forever-shifting but we're-all-in-this-together global pandemic.

Swirl

A final car story: it's a September 2020 morning, and I'm driving to the Cape to visit Paul. When my parents were alive, my husband and I made this hour-and-a-half trip many, many times. Today, I am alone. The sky over Boston is milky, murky from the West Coast fires; my horror at this unfathomable apocalypse fills me. I am bereft. I am tender. I am close to tears. I am alone, and suddenly, I miss my parents. "I miss my mother and father," I say out loud, both a statement and a question. Because this is what I always do when I am alone. I talk to myself out loud. I interpret myself to myself.

On Route 3 South, a complicated story tells itself simply and in installments: first, parked on the shoulder, an official-looking van idles, its flashers on. A mile or so later, a young Black man in a chartreuse, reflective vest spears trash. Thrusting his catch into a bright yellow plastic bag, he strides along the highway embankment, its late-summer grass parched and dusty and brown-green. Even at sixty miles an hour, I register his joy and his delight to move. To be outside and to be unencumbered. Further down the highway at maybe half-mile intervals lies his petrochemical harvest: one and then another and then another bulging, yellow bag. And then a few miles later appears another striding, grinning, young Black man and another depressing series of bulging, yellow bags.

I know, because a returning-citizen friend explained this to me, that my few-seconds-from-the-highway perception isn't wrong. Both young men likely consider this thankless, endless job to be an honor. And a joy.

But I am tender, vulnerable. I am alone. Deep sadness and, oh, hello, you again? anger wash over me, those disparate feelings tangled together like an impossible-to-brush-smooth snarl in my hair. Jim Crow and *The New Jim Crow*[75] and our nation's school-to-prison pipeline and cheap Black labor and SUVs with strapped-on bike racks and kayaks and tanned white arms lowering a back seat window to insouciantly toss out dirty diapers and Starbucks cups—I grok all of it. I feel all of it. I feel my own white arms holding the steering wheel. And at sixty miles an hour, I register my astonishment to experience this complicated, tangled snarl. "It was like eating a chocolate/vanilla soft-serve swirl," I will explain to my friend Ann later. "Every bite was a different combo of two distinct flavors."

To experience such snarled, swirled yet distinct emotions feels new. Apparently Spirit as Inner Teacher continues to guide my apprenticeship.

"Can't we do better than this?" I implore aloud, passing another yellow bag. "Why is this okay?"

But surely others wonder, too? Surely other travelers along this Pilgrims Highway—because that's what this stretch of highway is called—are asking, "Why is this okay?"

And I instantly grok this 1620 to 2020 moment on two-lane Pilgrims Highway; roadside pines and oaks speak of what came before. I grok every unrecorded story. I grok every page in every American history book. I take in wholeness; I take in a moment of All—what happens, sometimes, just before dinner, when I gratefully whisper, "All my relations."

My white arms hold the steering wheel. I hold this continent's history. I hold anger, sadness. I hold love, sea to shining sea love. I hold every living thing on this journey, all of us at this yellow-bag moment. I hold all who are at the very edge of this unfolding story. Poised.

"May you be ancestors worth descending from," Annie enjoins.

Let's try.

Appendix A

A (highly personalized) Quakerese Glossary:

A called meeting: Not a regularly scheduled meeting for worship but offered in times of stress, pain, tragedy—to collectively mourn.

Care of meeting: A Quaker quip: "Quakers didn't abolish the clergy; we abolished the laity!" At a silent, unprogrammed meeting for worship, in the waiting silence, anyone can access **that of God** within us. So, in a sense, everyone has care of meeting. One person is actually designated to have care of meeting, though; at FMC, this person is a member of **Ministry and Counsel**. Much like an elder, this person holds the space. This person also welcomes newcomers, makes announcements, and will intervene should a spoken message seem inappropriate, i.e. homophobic, racist, etc. At a Quaker memorial, when many people attending may have never attended a Quaker meeting before, it is especially important for the person who has care of meeting, who is not necessarily a member of M&C, to stand at the very beginning of the memorial to welcome everyone and explain a little about what is about to happen. And why.

"Eighteen to thirty-five-ish": At FMC, this phrase is often used to describe who's encouraged to join our Young Adult Friends group.

Elder: "Friends who feel exceptional concern for the deeper spiritual life of the meeting. They will also feel a concern for the encouragement and guidance of the vocal ministry. These, however, are but the primary qualifications to be looked for in elders. Ideally, they need, in addition, a considerable insight into character, an alert spiritual discernment, good judgment, and a fund of ready tact and open friendliness—all of these humbly dedicated to a deeply felt zeal for the spiritual growth of the Society, upheld and purified by the power of constant, watchful prayer" (*Faith and Practice of the North Carolina Yearly Meeting* [Conservative], 1983 Revision).

Experientially: "And this I knew experimentally," George Fox declared in 1647. Fox's seventeenth-century language and the more modern experientially both mean to know by listening to our Inner Teacher.

First Day: Because I have no problem with the days of the weeks being named after "pagan gods," I have never embraced the Quaker custom of calling Sunday **First Day**!

Hold in the Light: To pray for, to deeply connect with, to send positive, healing energy on behalf of someone.

Inner Teacher: Also known as the Inward Teacher, "small still voice," the Seed, Guide, Light, etc. That which is beyond ourselves, within us, and can be called upon through prayer, reflection.

Leading: To experience a nudge, a prompt from Spirit to do something, to faithfully act upon some possibly vague cue, outcome unknown. My leading to find Owen and Lynda began with no clear understanding of what this would entail; I just knew I was supposed to do it!

Opening: An insight, a deep understanding, a transcendent moment.

Meeting for worship: A regularly scheduled Quaker service that lasts for about an hour.

Ministry: Everyone has gifts. Everyone has access to the Divine. Everyone can be faithful, can listen to their Inner Teacher, and share their gifts. When I first attended Friends Meeting at Cambridge, for example, I noticed there was always a simple, homegrown flower arrangement on the table of the Friends Center's front hall, immediately visible when you entered. (I don't recall what appeared in the winter months—dried flowers, perhaps?) When I asked where these offerings came from, I learned that these endearing arrangements were an elderly woman's ministry. Everyone has gifts.

Ministry and Counsel committee: The group of people particularly tasked with a Quaker meeting's spiritual life. Members of M&C take turns having care of meeting and are responsible for other worship-sharing venues.

Read in tongues: a variation of listening in tongues; both readers and listeners are invited to mentally translate challenging language into words that speak to their condition.

Refiner's Fire: "Then after this did a pure fire appear in me; . . . and then the spiritual discerning came into me, by which I did discern my own thoughts, groans and sighs, and what it was that did veil me, and what it was that did open me." George Fox, *Journal of George Fox,* 1647, pp. 14, 15.

Like many early Friends, Fox was referencing the Bible—which his seventeenth-century readers and his listeners would immediately recognize. In this case: Malachi 3:2-3 ESV: "But who can endure the day of his coming, and who can stand when he appears? For he is like a refiner's fire and like fullers' soap. He will sit as a refiner and purifier of silver, and he will purify the sons of Levi and refine them like gold and silver, and they will bring offerings in righteousness to the Lord." Amen.

Resident Friend: At Friends Meeting at Cambridge, this has been a full-time, paid position with housing in our Friends Center provided as well. Both an administrative and ministerial position, at this writing, FMC is examining this challenging, multiple responsibilities role.

Ritual-wary: Early Friends, filled with the zeal of a living, present-tense experience of the Divine, shunned ritual and its potential to allow any ceremony to replace deep, inward, unfolding-in-real-time experience. Filled with that zeal as I write this, I understand their concerns. I get it. I also know that there have been times in my life when a physical object has allowed me to more deeply center and to be more fully present. Years ago, for example, about the same time I'd been hired as my Quaker meeting's First Day School Coordinator, i.e. its religious education director, a cotton, peach-colored scarf randomly appeared on my front hall's coat rack. When no one claimed that scarf and called upon to sometimes engage in very challenging and difficult conversations with meeting parents, I began to wear that cast-off as if my vestment. Feeling its softness around my neck reminded me that I'd been entrusted to listen with love and compassion and to seek Spirit's guidance before I spoke—rather than to natter on about something I'd learned in an early childhood development class at Wheelock College.

"Speak to the center of the room": Pre-worship-sharing advice, a reminder that we're trying to share what's on our heart and not giving advice.

Speaks to [my] condition: Words or actions that align with my inner experience, my inward sense—resonate.

Spirit: Because the word *God* is so freighted for so many people I love, I use the word *Spirit* instead of *God*. For me, Inner Teacher, the Ineffable, Wholeness, or other expressions of the Divine would serve. *Spirit* seems to resonate with more people, though.

State of Society Report: Every year, in order to send this required report to New England Yearly Meeting, FMC takes a hard, honest look at itself. Every year, sometimes silently, sometimes out loud at meeting for business, I rail against what seems a meaningless ritual—and every year, after we've collectively agreed that our final document to be close-enough-true about meeting, I am so grateful to have once again participated in this FMC-reflective process.

That of God: "And this is the word of the Lord God to you all, and a charge to you all in the presence of the living God: be patterns, be examples in all countries, places, islands, nations, wherever you come, that your carriage and life may preach among all sorts of people, and to them; then you will come to walk cheerfully over the world, answering that of God in every one." George Fox, 1656

The *Inward Holy* might be another way to describe **that of God**. I'm comfortable with *Soul*, too—although I haven't heard many other Quakers use this language.

What seems important are two things:

One: Fox used the verb *answering*, i.e. as we're cheerfully walking over the world, we listen. We're open. We're acknowledging that others are also Children of God. (I cringe whenever anyone gets this foundational Fox quote wrong and instead says *speaking to that of God*. Or *seeking*. Nope.)

Two: *in every one*. Whatever language we use to identify this ineffable **that of God**, Fox is saying everyone has it. No exceptions.

Way opens: "The serendipitous unfolding of God's will for a person or community." Alex Levering Kern

What comes through you: An idea, a question, a line of poetry, a piece of writing, or vocal ministry that comes from a beyond-ourselves place—and not just "something I'd read in *The New York Times*."

Witness (verb): To show up, make a statement by one's presence—no actual words required.

(noun) A person showing up, saying with their body, their presence, "This is what I believe."

Worship-sharing: A worshipful mode of group reflection in which participants speak once and "to the center of the room," and the facilitator allows space between reflections in order to allow everyone to take in what has just been offered.

Appendix B

Faithfulness Groups Workshop Handout

By Jennifer Hogue, Friends Meeting at Cambridge, and Marcelle Martin, author of *Our Life is Love*
(https://awholeheart.com)

Evoking questions are designed to help one another notice more fully the movement of the Spirit. They assist a person in exploring their deep responses and inner knowing about a situation. This is different from questions of fact (outward information) or questions that elicit intellectual analysis or reflection. Evoking questions often invite a person to use imagination or to describe images, metaphors, feelings, sensations, or bodily awareness. Some questions ask the person to "look at God" and to sense how the Divine is present with them in the present or in particular situations and concerns.

Example:
Jess is discerning about a possible work, service, or witness opportunity.

Factual questions:
- What would be your start date?
- Who else is involved?
- Did you say you were offered this opportunity two years ago?

Reflective/analytical questions:
- What new skills would be required?
- How might this impact future career or witness opportunities?

Evoking questions:
- How do you sense that God/Spirit/the Light/Love is present in this opportunity?
- Have you received any nudges, messages, or signs about this possibility?
- What might be your biggest challenges or opportunities to grow in this work?
- When you imagine doing this work, how does your body and your breathing feel?
- How do you feel when you think about who you would be serving?
- Does this opportunity feel like a temptation? If so, why?

Mini Faithfulness Trio Format

Each person has twelve minutes as the focus of the group.
1. **Four minutes to speak about recent efforts to be faithful** in a particular area of life or in service or witness or in following a leading or a call to some kind of ministry. (Or up to four minutes; if you finish early you can spend more time on the second step.)
2. **Four minutes for the listeners to ask evoking questions** about what has been shared. One person writes these down.
3. **Four minutes for the speaker to respond** to one of the questions.
4. **Two minutes for worship** in between focus individuals.

Faithfulness Group Meeting Format

Role of convener—this role rotates (one convener/meeting). This person will open and close each meeting, keep time, moderate the discussion as needed, attending to whether it is following the desired intent, atmosphere, and attitude. The focus should be on the presenter in an atmosphere of holy accompaniment, and the basic intent is to be open and responsive to the Spirit.

Role of presenter—this role rotates (two presenters/meeting). This person has about fifteen minutes to share about specific incidents, inner movements, and concerns related to their efforts to be faithful. Deciding what to present calls for prayerful reflection ahead of time.

Note—One person should not serve as both convener and presenter during a given meeting.

SCHEDULE (approximate)
- **Opening**—convener reminds group about intended focus and attitude
- **Opening worship**—about five minutes
- **First presentation**—up to fifteen minutes. (Group listens silently to the presentation; at the end, the presenter can be asked to speak about their prayer in relationship to what has been shared if this has not yet been mentioned.)
- **Brief factual questions of clarification** (if necessary)—about two minutes
- **Silent prayer, reflection**—about two minutes

- **Evoking questions and exploration**—about thirty-five minutes
- **Break**—five minutes
- **Second presentation**—up to fifteen minutes. (Group listens silently to the presentation; at the end, the presenter can be asked to speak about their prayer in relationship to what has been shared if this has not yet been mentioned.)
- **Brief factual questions of clarification** (if necessary)—about two minutes
- **Silent prayer, reflection**—about two minutes
- **Evoking questions and exploration**—about thirty-five minutes
- **Process of meeting**—five minutes*
- **Closing worship**—two to five minutes

*Evaluating and processing the faithfulness group meeting—the convener asks the group to reflect on the meeting. Some useful questions include:

- Was there a sense of prayerful presence in the group?
- What facilitated that or got in the way?
- Was there a sense of spiritual discernment happening for the presenter? How well did we stay focused on the presenter and their relationship with Spirit?
- Were there any places we seemed to be off track (i.e. too much problem-solving, overly analytical, etc.)

Appendix C

"On Studying Sacred Texts," by Judith Offer
[Used with permission]

Do not go alone into the Word.
Take someone with you to the place
Where all questions are answered
But all answers are questions.
Travel in a truth-seeking troupe; someone
Is bound to know which verse you're on
And you can reel each other back in
When you slide off the Page.

The Book of Endless Light
Is trackless, sometimes steep, verbose or
Thicketed with metaphor. Each flower
Is the first of its kind, and the last.
You may be frightened at times by
The unspeakable beauty.
Terror can unmake your concentration,
So you do not hear the meanings
Bubble to the surface. You can die of thirst,
With springs everywhere.

If what you are traveling into
Is all the Truth that ever was,
Obviously, it is too much for one puny human.
Be at least two of you:
A teacher is the preferred companion,
Or a lover will suffice,
But avoid authorities, and pessimists,
And anyone else who thrives on comparison,
Or who has never studied a dust mote in the sun.

It is written. Do not go alone into the Word.
Thus, be a minimum of two of you.
And take your angels, if they'll go. Also,
Take the memories of those who have gone before,
Yet can form words to speak of it.
When you have gathered all you can;
Teachers, lovers, seekers,
Angels and memories,
Take a deep breath, take someone's hand,
And take my blessing. And go.

Acknowledgments

First, I must acknowledge this: On June 7, 2022, my fierce, brilliant, multi-talented sister, Deborah Wild, died of pancreatic cancer, a scant ten weeks after learning her diagnosis. Extroverted, hilarious, generous with her time and her extraordinary organizational skills, Deborah was often at the center of wherever she found herself. Yet as she, herself, acknowledged, "I am 'acquainted with grief.'" Deborah's wise counsel, her lived experiences of shame and loss, and her insights about the family we present-tense share undergird *Strands*.

And then this: On August 11, 2024, Paul Wild, my best friend, died when his congenital myasthenia, the lifetime condition he'd shared with Ben, finally took its toll. Single, an introvert, an outrageous raconteur (No, he had not been on the "Andrea Doria" when it collided with another ship in Nantucket Sound!), his huge circle of friends and our diminished family miss his wit, his barbed rejoinders, his generous laugh. We mourn him yet remind ourselves, over and over, how challenging his last year had been.

Thus, *never-been-so* continues. Never before has *family* meant such piercing love shadowed by such searing grief! Never before have I ever been so close to Ben! And never before has this cruel, gorgeous world been so complicated.

So, never before have I been so grateful for my four daughters. Thank you, Melissa, Hope, Allison, and Christina. "Your children are either the center of your life or they aren't. And the rest is commentary," Calvin Trillin once noted. You four are the rock-solid center of my life.

Such gratitude for David Myers. Like my parents' song declares, "I love you truly."

For grandchildren, Dmitri, Sasha, Ruby, Sam, Lilian, Amy, and now, Arlo. What unconditional, no-exceptions joy you are! Thank you, precious ones, for keeping me keenly aware of the *fewcha*.

For Jeremy, Vita, Jess, Garen, Tigran, dearly departed Chris, Mike, Dave, Kristian, Dustin, Judy, Tina, Tyler, Brielle, Cameron, Steve, Hannah, Abby, John, Donna, Jennifer, Elizabeth, Jim, Peter Wild, and Christina Ta: I hold you all close to my heart. "We are family."

For my dear friends whose fingerprints are all over this book. Some have been named, like Eric Beutner, Yani Burgos, Owen Cardwell, Minga Claggett-Borne, Ann Foster, Chris Jorgenson, Lynn Lazar, Diana Lopez, Wendy Sandford, Dinah Starr, Kevin Thomas, Kim West, and Lynda Woodruff. And some dear friends, like Lissa Gifford, who'd mailed me a photocopy of that referenced, apt Rilke poem years ago, I now publicly thank. Like Susan Bunch Blanchard, Nancy Bloom, Kathleen Bruce, Linda Garrison, Mary Gilbert, Sherry Gordon, Martha Irwin, Jane Jackson, Eva Lloyd Jones, Diana Marcil, Delia Marshall, Susan Lloyd McGarry, Jan Nisenbaum, Buzzy Olan, Hillary Pannier, Janey Snyder, Lili Schwan-Rosenwald, and Pam Thayer. Like the Plum

Village song goes, "You have given me such treasures." Like the piles of wonderful books Kate Cloud supplied during this pandemic. All of you are within these pages. Thank you.

For my not-forgotten ancestors: Paul and Florence Wild, Lilian Horrie, Kay Salwitz, Amy Zlotnick; thank you for your stories and our enriching times together. You are my portal to the past; where I now perch on that proverbial, eternal timeline is more clear because of you.

Thank you, Wednesday night sharing circle for the wisdom, the laughs and the tears, for your "goodwill, support, and healing," for allowing me to become a member of another family, and for showing me what being human means. Thank you, Akira, Ajamu, Berk, Brian, Carlos, Chris, Glenn, George, James, Jennifer, Joe, Joel, Joseph, John B, the two John Cs, Julia, Kathy W., Lynn, Maeve, Mark, Mary Lynn, Mehmet, Nesto, Patrick, Patty, Rick, Rodney, Ron, Rudy, Tony, and Warner. Although some circle members are no longer with us, I feel your spirit every Wednesday night.

Our fossil-fuels voluntary tax group makes me so happy: Susan Davies and Rick Talkov, Chris, Minga, and Jonathon Vogel-Borne.

A special place in my heart for my gifted teacher, Annie Hoffman, whose befitting poetry references and in-the-moment metaphors make me gasp with delight—or giggle. So grateful for my sangha-mates, too: Adelaide, Anne, Judy, Lisa, Lynn, Mary Elizabeth, Miriam, Nancy, Pattie, Paula, Rachel, and Sandy. Typing your names makes me smile.

For all the Somerville-based community activists, gardeners, artists, musicians, and writers who have made this city a wonderful place to live and work and raise children, thank you.

Before moving on to specific people for their specific contributions to *Strands*, a hymn of thanksgiving for Constance Kehoe, my freshman-year English instructor at Boston's Wheelock College. At our first conference she'd asked me, "Are you going to use that brain of yours, or are you going to just rely on charm your whole life?"

Strands could not have been written without my iterative Nurturing Faithfulness Group. Thank you, Charlotte Wood-Harrington, Elise Spinguel, Jane Threefoot, Mari Rufo, and Nora Sullivan. You are my rod and my staff.

Thank you, Eric Muhr, for your faith in *Strands* and for your steady, patient guidance throughout this publishing process. What an honor to be published by Barclay Press!

I am so grateful that five people I deeply admire, Alexander Levering Kern, Marcelle Martin, Zenaida Peterson, and Nancy Sowell, for graciously and generously agreeing to read *Strands* and craft such beautiful endorsements! Thank you.

Thank you, Oliver House, Yates County History Center, Penn Yan, New York, for permission to use your hair wreath photograph.

Much gratitude, Polly Atwood, for your thoughtful and careful editing of the section dealing with FMC as a group.

That you reappeared in my life, Laurie Wolfe, just when ready to delve more deeply into my Shaker Village Work Group experience, seems a miracle!

Many thanks to Representative Erika Uyterhoeven for tracking down the status of the Somerville Retirement Board divestment process.

And I will end this list the same way I often begin worship by acknowledging "all my relations." Especially my neighborhood's talented mockingbird.

Notes from Text

1 *Wild Edge of Sorrow: Rituals of Renewal and the Sacred Work of Grief* by Francis Weller, North Atlantic Books, 2015, p. 4

2 Weller, p. 47

3 Jet Beads: Jet as a gemstone became fashionable during the reign of Queen Victoria. https://en.wikipedia.org/wiki/Jet_(gemstone)

4 David Brooks, *The Second Mountain,* Random House, 2019. https://www.bookon9.com/romance/14587/14587_21.html

5 Weller, p.7

6 Frank and Lillian Gilbreth were pioneer efficiency experts. http://www.thegilbreths.com

7 *The Age of Fable* by Thomas Bullfinch, illustrated by Kenneth Bogert, Rodale Press, 1948, p. 98

8 *Care of the Soul: A Guide for Cultivating Depth and Sacredness in Everyday Life* by Thomas Moore, Harper Perennial, 1992, p. 107

9   Ibid, p. 199

10 *The Testimony of the Soul* by Rufus Jones, The Macmillan Company, 1936, p. 5

11 Ibid, p.21

12 *Conjectures of a Guilty Bystander* by Thomas Merton, Image Books edition 1968 (by special arrangement with Doubleday & Company, Inc.). Image Books edition published February 1968. The first paragraph of the quote is on p. 156, the second paragraph is on p. 158.

13 From the back cover of *Daddy-Long Legs*, Jean Webster, Random House, 2011: "The Looking Glass Library series offers up yesterday's finest children's books, with introductions by today's foremost writers. Each book is among the best of its kind, written with skill and imaginative truth by authors who turned stories for children into great works of literature."

14 Jones, p. 208

15 Weller, p. 32

16 The entire quote from a George Fox letter written in 1656 is: "And this is the word of the Lord God to you all, and a charge to you all in the presence of the living God: be patterns, be examples in all countries, places, islands, nations, wherever you come, that your carriage and life may preach among all sorts of people, and to them; then you will come to walk cheerfully over the world, answering that of God in every one."

17 Weller, p. 54

18 *Meeting Jesus Again for the First Time: The Historical Jesus*

and the Heart of Contemporary Faith by Marcus J. Borg, Harper One, 1994

19 *The Five Invitations: Discovering What Death Can Teach Us About Living Fully* by Frank Ostaseski, Flatiron Books, 2017, p. 32

20 John Calvi is a gifted healer and a released Friend, i.e. his Putney, Vermont, Quaker meeting supports his ministry in some way.

21 "Be Still and Cool": A letter to Lady Claypole, daughter of Oliver Cromwell, *Journal*, ed. Nickalls, p. 346f

22 Weller, p. 110

23 Easter Egg: "A message, image, or feature hidden in a video game, film, or other, usually electronic, medium." https://en.wikipedia.org/wiki/Easter_egg_(media)

24 Mothers Out Front: https://www.mothersoutfront.org

25 Currently, this divestment process, which involves a home rule petition, stalls at the state level—although on September 10, 2021, Harvard University announced it was divesting from fossil fuels.

26 As quoted in my memoir, *Way Opens: A Spiritual Journey*, p. 184

27 Martin Luther King Jr. "New York Times" https://www.nytimes.com/2017/12/22/opinion/martin-luther-king-christmas.html

28 The entire quote: "Give over thine own willing, give over thy own running, give over thine own desiring

to know or be anything and sink down to the seed which God sows in the heart, and let that grow in thee and be in thee and breathe in thee and act in thee; and thou shalt find by sweet experience that the Lord knows that and loves and owns that, and will lead it to the inheritance of Life, which is its portion." Isaac Penington, 1661

29 Voluntary Tax Formula: https://www.mounttobyfriends.org/action/voluntary-carbon-tax-witness/

30 Cosecha website: https://www.lahuelga.com/index

31 Moore, p. 111

32 Public Charge: "Public charge," as defined by the former Immigration and Naturalization Service (INS, now U.S. Citizenship and Immigration Services, or USCIS), refers to an individual who is likely to become "primarily dependent on the government for subsistence, as demonstrated by either the receipt of public cash assistance for income maintenance or institutionalization for long-term care at government expense." The term describes people who cannot support themselves and who depend on benefits that provide cash—such as Supplemental Security Income (SSI) or Temporary Assistance for Needy Families (TANF)—for their income. An individual who is likely at any time to become a public charge is inadmissible to the United States and ineligible to become a lawful permanent resident. [National Immigration Law Center] https://www.nilc.org/issues/economic-support/public-charge-overview/]

33 The meaning of Om from the Verywellfit website: https://www.verywellfit.com "Om is a very simple sound with a complex meaning. It is the whole universe coalesced into a single word, representing the union of mind, body, and spirit that is at the heart of yoga. Often chanted three times at the start and at the finish of a yoga session, the sound of om is actually three syllables: a, u, and m."

34 *From Long Ago and Many Lands: Stories for Children Told Anew* by Sophia L. Fahs, Beacon Press, 1948

35 Grok: to understand profoundly through intuition or empathy. First used in *Stranger in a Strange Land* by Robert A. Heinlein, 1961

36 "The Doctrine of Discovery established a spiritual, political, and legal justification for colonization and seizure of land not inhabited by Christians. It has been invoked since Pope Alexander VI issued the Papal Bull 'Inter Caetera' in 1493. The Papal decree aimed to justify Christian European explorers' claims on land and waterways they allegedly discovered, and promote Christian domination and superiority." https://upstanderproject.org/firstlight/doctrine

37 Rabbett Before Horses Strickland (Red Cliff Band of Anishinaabe, born 1949) *Creation Story*, 2009, oil on canvas, collection, Tweed Museum of Art, University of Minnesota Duluth, Alice Tweed Tuohy Foundation Purchase Fund, D2009.28

38 Jones, p.151

39 Quaker Peace Testimony, 1660

40 *On the Brink of Everything: Grace, Gravity and Getting Old* by Parker Palmer, Berrett-Koehler Publishers, Inc., 2018

41 Bulfinch, p. 22

42 Many of us read Peggy McIntosh's essay, "Unpacking the Invisible Knapsack" in "Peace and Freedom Magazine," 1989, and Tim Wise's *White Like Me: Reflections on Race from a Privileged Son*, Soft Skull Press, 2004

43 Kenneth Jones and Tema Okun's "White Supremacy Culture." http://www.cwsworkshop.org/PARC_site_B/dr-culture.html

44 https://www.workers.org/2006/us/somerville5-0928/

45 From *Mary Don't You Weep*, a spiritual from before the Civil War.

46 "Let us then try what Love will do." William Penn, 1693

47 "Stan Freberg Presents the United States of America Volume One: The Early Years, " came out in 1961; my first experience of brilliant and sometimes horrifyingly hilarious satire.

48 Zillow says that house was built in 1912; my father said 1890. I'm going with my father.

49 *Tikkun Olam*: Hebrew for "world repair" and has come to mean social action and the pursuit of social justice.

50 Weller, p. 68

51 Ibid, p. 59, quoting Michael Ventura

52 Hugh Barbour, Resident Friend at FMC during the

early nineties, used those words when giving a forum on "The Sermon on the Mount" and "The Sermon on the Plain."

53 Weller, p. 57

54 Wendy Sanford's *These Walls Between Us: A Memoir of Friendship Across Race and Class*, published by She Writes Press, 2021, tells of her deep, emergent, touching friendship, woven over decades, with Mary Norman, an African American woman who did domestic work for Wendy's owning-class, white family.

55 "United for a Fair Economy challenges the concentration of wealth and power that corrupts democracy, deepens the racial divide and tears communities apart. We use popular economics education, trainings, and creative communications to support social movements working for a resilient, sustainable and equitable economy." https://www.faireconomy.org

56 See *Fit for Freedom, Not For Friendship: Quakers, African Americans, and the Myth of Racial Justice* by Donna McDaniel and Vanessa Julye or "When Quakers Were the Karens," by Elizabeth Cazden, *Friends Journal*, January 2021.

57 Many of us read Isabel Wilkerson's *Caste: The Origins of Our Discontent*, published by Random House in 2020. It's devastating. Brilliant. And right on.

58 Shaker Village Work Group: https://www.shakermuseum.us/collection/shaker-village-work-group/

59 25 Traits of the Beloved Community: https://www.r2hub.org/library/25-traits-of-the-beloved-community

60 From the Circle's flyer

61 https://vimeo.com/4262767

62 Kimmerer, p. 318

63 Ibid, p. 319

64 Ibid, p. 332

65 Ibid, p. 319

66 Ibid, p. 332

67 Blog post, "Heinrich von Ofterdingen: The Tale of the Blue Flower," Erwida Maulia, January 7, 2013

68 Kimmerer, pp. 335-6.

69 John Woolman's Journal: 12th day, 6th month, first week, 1763. Aptly, the entire quote reads, "Love was the first motion, and then a concern arose to spend some time with the Indians [sic], that I might feel and understand their life and the spirit they live in, if haply I might receive some instruction from them, or they be in any degree helped forward by my following the leadings of Truth among them."

70 Weller, p. 18

71 Ibid, p. 74

72 "Title Poem," by Rainer Maria Rilke, *Selected Poems of Rainer Maria Rilke: A Translation from the German* by Robert Bly, Harper & Row, New York, 1981, p. 111

73 Weller, p. 68

74 Quaker Peace Testimony, 1660.

75 *The New Jim Crow: Mass Incarceration in the Age of Colorblindness* by Michelle Alexander (New Press, 2010) links systemic racism and our prison system and how the war on drugs targeted young Black men.

Notes from Illustrations

76 *Braiding Sweetgrass: Indigenous Wisdom, Scientific Knowledge and the Teachings of Plants* by Robin Wall Kimmerer, Milkweed Editions, 2013, p. 327

77 Weller, quoting James Hillman, p. xx

78 Weller, p. 153

79 Weller, p. 110

80 Weller, p. 5

www.ingramcontent.com/pod-product-compliance
Lightning Source LLC
Chambersburg PA
CBHW010051200426
43193CB00059B/2920